KÄTHE KOLLWITZ

GRAPHICS

POSTERS

DRAWINGS

KÄTHE KOLLWITZ

GRAPHICS
POSTERS
DRAWINGS

EDITED BY RENATE HINZ

FOREWORD BY LUCY R. LIPPARD

TRANSLATED FROM THE GERMAN

BY RITA AND ROBERT KIMBER

PANTHEON BOOKS   NEW YORK

Grateful acknowledgment is made to the following for permission to reprint previously
published material:

University of California at Riverside, Art Galleries: For bibliography by Marion Buzzard
and Adrienne R. Long, from Käthe Kollwitz, Prints, Drawings, Sculpture, *1978,*
a catalogue edited with an introduction by Françoìse Forster-Hahn. Permission to reprint the
bibliography is granted by the Regents of the University of California, Riverside.
Galerie St. Etienne: For quotation from a statement by Käthe Kollwitz,
p. ix, courtesy Galerie St. Etienne, New York. Translation Copyright © 1981 by
Martha Kearns.

Library of Congress Cataloging in Publication Data

Kollwitz, Käthe, 1867-1945.

Käthe Kollwitz : graphics, posters, drawings.

Bibliography: p.

1. Kollwitz, Käthe, 1867-1945. I. Hinz, Renate.

II. Title.

N6888.K62A4 1982   760'.092'4   81-47272

ISBN 0-394-51948-5   AACR2

ISBN 0-394-74878-6 (pbk.)

Manufactured in the United States of America

First American Edition

CONTENTS

KOLLWITZ: CHIAROSCURO

A rt for the average spectator need not be shallow. Of course he has no objection to the trite—but it is also true that he would accept true art if it were simple enough. I thoroughly agree that there must be understanding between the artist and the people. In the best ages of art that has always been the case. Genius can probably run on ahead and seek out new ways. But the good artists who follow after genius—and I count myself among these—have to restore the lost connection once more. A pure studio art is unfruitful and frail, for anything that does not form living roots—why should it exist at all?[1]
—*Käthe Kollwitz*, 1916

This statement by Kollwitz sounds simple, just as her art appears to be simple. Yet both her words and her work raise some of the most complex questions about the role of the artist in society, questions that have neither been answered nor forgotten since her death. As we enter still another period of social turmoil, the time seems ripe to find a new context in which to consider Kollwitz's art, in order to jolt it out of the clichés in which it has long been confined, and free it to become not a monument, but a model for progressive artists.[2]

Although there is a good deal of discussion these days in America about the possibilities and development of a socially responsive art, Kollwitz's name is rarely raised. In the midst of the antifascist struggles of the 1930s and '40s, she was compared worldwide to Daumier, Goya, and even Rembrandt. In the '50s, with the triumph of modernism, cold war, and McCarthyism, her work became "illustrational," "obvious," "emotional," and "literary." Kollwitz's art-world invisibility in the midst of the political upheavals of the late 1960s is far more problematic. She has in some curious way been removed from history. Like John Heartfield and a few others, she is remembered primarily in the framework of Left culture rather than within the "high art" mainstream.

The reasons for this neglect are rooted in several calculated and/or unconscious notions that have dominated art history and criticism in the postwar period. They in turn are based on a series of false dichotomies that reinforce the myth of the artist as either above it all or below it all—either the isolated genius at the frontiers of formal innovation (which accounts for the military notion of the "avant-garde") or the powerless outcast taking care of society's less important chores.[3] Kollwitz, on the other hand, was very much part of it all—"it all" being quite simply life. She firmly integrated her social experience, her ethics, and her politics with her art. This in itself was enough to set her apart from most of her contemporaries—and to confuse the chroniclers.

Like many important women artists, Kollwitz was a synthesizer. This is not, unfortunately, a much-respected role if one sees art history in terms of great linear leaps forward. When I was writing a book on the young sculptor Eva Hesse,[4] I was asked by artist friends of hers to be sure *not* to make her a synthesizer, because that would diminish her historical importance. Yet Hesse, like Kollwitz, had a need to dispel polarities, to fuse expressionism and simplicity, to heal wounds, to balance contradictions.

Such synthesizing is perhaps the product of isolation. The loner (and most women artists have had little choice but to be loners) remains outside of major art movements and forgoes the role of leader within a set style that is so dear to the hearts of historians. Kollwitz was a loner not because she was rebelling against the mainstream but because she was extremely clear about her own priorities. Consequently, she has had to be forced into inappropriate or irrelevant categories to make it into the history books at all. For instance, Carl Zigrosser's book on Expressionist prints introduces Kollwitz through the influence of Ernst Barlach's woodcuts, though this occurred only in 1920, when she had been producing her own successful and mature work for over twenty years.[5] Another ploy is to place her by gender. In a 1957 book on German art, she appears near the end, under prints, with painter Paula Modersohn-Becker, with whom she had little in common except sex and occasional subject matter. According to William S. Lieberman, the two women "stand between Post-Impressionism and the Expressionists. . . . Kollwitz, almost entirely a graphic artist, passed from the influence of Klinger to a more expressive style.[6] Illustrative, somewhat sentimental expositions on proletarian themes constitute her early work. Later her protest and sympathy became less particularized and more direct."[7]

This is not the place to analyze oversimplifications, and Kollwitz has also received her share of intelligent coverage in monographs, if not in general histories. Yet even her admirers tend to fall into the same trap as her patronizers by considering her art in terms of black and white, either/or. Ulrich Weisner, for instance, wrote that "it was a human rather than a political concern which led to the creation of works determined by politics."[8] Such statements ignore the fact that political concerns *are* human concerns, that what art and politics have in common is their capacity to move us. The polarization of personal and political has led to the current and disastrous neutralization of art within the international avant-garde; it is accompanied (or caused) by the commodification of socially uninvolved art and a systematic exclusion of socially involved art from modernist art history. It is this syndrome within which Kollwitz is seen as a rather quaint figure whose art and values were embarrassingly "uncool." This is the way I was conditioned to look at her work. Her very authenticity strikes a jarring note in the fashion-oriented art world. Her art and her life were so focused, inward, exacting, and politically correct that they can seem an impregnable monolith. For a large segment of the contemporary art

audience, the combined formal and emotional integrity of Kollwitz's prints and sculpture are almost impossible to see.

This is not merely a matter of style nor of generations, but of context and values, the latter a factor too rarely considered in art criticism. Kollwitz's passion and compassion separated her from the harsh satires and desperate inventiveness of her younger colleagues during the Weimar Republic. The belligerent brilliance of Dada, for instance, was probably anathema to her. Yet she who had lost her son in the war shared certain significant values with those younger men who had lost their youth in the war. Richard Huelsenbeck might have been describing Kollwitz's work in the First German Dada Manifesto, despite the fact that he began by insulting all Expressionists:

Art in execution and direction is dependent on the time in which it lives, and artists are creatures of their epoch. The highest art will be that which in its conscious content presents the thousandfold problems of the day, the art which has been visibly shattered by the explosions of the last week, which is forever trying to collect its limbs after yesterday's crash. The best and most extraordinary artists will be those who every hour snatch the tatters of their bodies out of the frenzied cataracts of life, who, with bleeding hands and hearts, hold fast to the intelligence of their time.[9]

Contemporary artists working from exactly the opposite direction, under the prevailing notion that art is timeless, classless, and detached, tend to feel so helpless in the face of political events that they retreat into individualism and voluntary isolation, away from audience, life, and history itself, leaving the control of their art in the hands of those who use it in ways quite alien to its original purposes. It has in fact been fashionable for the past two decades to declare that art is functionless—and by extension, meaningless. Kollwitz was aware of this attitude in her day as well. In the 1920s she wrote: "I have received a commission to make a poster against war. That is a task that makes me happy. Some may say a thousand times that this is not pure art . . . but as long as I can work, I want to be effective with my art."[10]

Thus it is also time to rehabilitate the two words most often used pejoratively to describe Kollwitz's work—"sentimental" and "propaganda." The original meaning of sentimental—"characterized by or exhibiting refined or elevated feeling"—is far more appropriate to the power of her prints and sculptures than the current meaning—"addicted to indulgence in superficial emotion." The latter may apply to many of her imitators, but the dramatic depth and formal weight of Kollwitz's own images are carved in the flesh and bone of her subjects' lives. Similarly, propaganda means "devoting oneself to the propagation of some creed or doctrine"—an apt enough goal for an artist whose task is communication. Yet Kollwitz's critics and supporters tend to bounce back and forth between denying that she made propaganda and endowing the word with its original power. For instance, where Francis Henry Taylor wrote in the '40s: "The drawings and prints of Käthe Kollwitz are too fervent and sincere to be classed as propaganda,"[55] Leonard Baskin wrote in 1959: "All art is propaganda. All art is tendentious. The communication of an idea is an act of propaganda";[12] and Carl Zigrosser said: "Propaganda, then, is special pleading of a sort."[13]

Muriel Rukeyser's moving poem on Kollwitz includes one line in a man's voice, a remark which was actually made to the poet by an acquaintance: "Kollwitz? She's too black and white." In this terse comment are buried several levels of criticism. The most obvious concerns the fact that the graphic arts are considered "minor" efforts compared to the large scale and monumental ego (and, not incidentally, monetary value) supposedly intrinsic to "major" fine arts mediums such as oil paint and bronze. Prints, and woodcuts in particular, are a venerable populist medium—so direct and simple that they can finally be a greater challenge to the subtle artist than the subtler media. Kollwitz was a perfectionist, and spent as much time on her prints as most artists do on huge canvases. The Liebknecht memorial woodcut was preceded by twenty-four line drawings, composition studies, an etching, and a lithograph. The *War* series, dated 1922–23, took much longer: "No one would guess that these seven woodcuts of medium size encompass a work of many years, and yet it is so."[14] Early on, Kollwitz had made a conscious choice to work with graphics because of their accessibility. This decision is also relevant to progressive artists today working with book and magazine art, posters, video, and other mass-production techniques for similar reasons. At the same time, Kollwitz's choice of a "colorless" and volumetric medium must also have been temperamental. As Baskin, himself a sculptor and graphic artist, has written, "The blandishment of colors, the inevitable sensuousness of fat oil or sparkling water paints were alien to her needs. She dwelt in a world of blacks and whites."[15]

The starkness of such contrasts may have been most compatible with Kollwitz's content, but "too black and white," as in Rukeyser's line, implies banality—"we know all about that stuff"—which in turn stems from commercial notions of novelty and planned obsolescence in the art market. It also testifies to a lack of understanding on the part of the middle-class audience that buys and "appreciates" art—an impatient, elitist miscomprehension of the social contexts in which artists like Kollwitz work. We already "know all that stuff" about nudes and landscapes and colored stripes and steel spheres too—or so we think. But these are acceptable subjects for "high art" today, whereas death, war, motherhood, and economics are "clichés."

The proof of Kollwitz's authenticity as a propagator is the fact that whereas most socially involved artists today use (and need to use) a combination of words and images to communicate to an audience that doesn't expect a message from art, Kollwitz's wordless prints and drawings are as politically effective as her posters, or even more so. Ironically, it is due to this success that she is so often called a "mere propagandist." In her white-on-black woodcuts, the figures loom out of a darkness that seems as historical as it is spatial. She used this crisp, unrelenting medium to document equally relentless conditions. Even when the dramatic gesture or movement is paramount, the subject's intensity is carried by *volume,* transmitted by lights and darks, black and white.

Her politics emerged from her social life, her gut, her heart, her historical awareness, and merged with the forms of the human bodies that were the vehicles for her beliefs. She dealt with tragedy, not pathos, though tragedy was not usually associated with the lives of working-class people. The sheer *weight* of this lived experience provides an enduring metaphor for Kollwitz's art. Her formal strategies were integrated with her content. There are no weak spots in her shapes or compositions; like her figures, they are compact and earthbound, held together by a suggested solidity/solidarity. In the person of each weary woman, bowed under oppression she is helpless to affect directly, is the hidden courage and endurance that permits her to survive and will eventually permit her to fight back.

There was also an evangelical component to Kollwitz's responses that can be traced to her attachment to her father, a committed social democrat, and her grandfather, a reform preacher. She often mentioned "a duty to serve" through her art. As a child she was fascinated by the bodies and faces of waterfront laborers in her hometown, by their "native rugged simplicity . . . a grandness of manner, a breadth to their lives."[16] However sincere, such romantic attitudes verge on a patronizing classism. In addition, she felt a level of intolerance for her own class that these days would probably be chalked up to "middle-class guilt." "Middle-class people held no appeal for me at all," she recalled. "Bourgeois life as a whole seemed to me pedantic." And as for the "upper-class educated person," "he's not natural or true; he's not honest, and he's not a human being in every sense of the word."[17]

With age, however, Kollwitz learned to become more tolerant. Living with her doctor husband in Berlin's poorest district, she was "gripped by the full force of the proletarian's fate. Unsolved problems such as prostitution and unemployment grieved and tormented me, and contributed to my feeling that I must keep on with my studies of the lower classes. And portraying them again and again opened a safety valve for me; it made life bearable."[18] Life in Berlin offered the practice to fuse with the theories of her Königsberg girlhood. One of the most moving aspects of Kollwitz's biography is the evolution of her intimate and utterly natural relationships with the women whose lives and sorrows she came to share, depict, objectify into searing symbols of injustice. Yet she agreed with her sister Lise, who once "made a point which is for the most part ignored when many people assert that my one subject is always the lot of the unfortunate. Sorrow isn't confined to social misery."[19]

It is the integration of the physical, emotional, and social that makes Kollwitz an important artist. As Rukeyser put it: "The faces of sufferers/in the street, in dailiness,/their lives showing/through their bodies/ a look as of music/the revolutionary look/that says I am in the world/to change the world."[20] Kollwitz's sole interest as an artist was the human figure. "The working-class woman," she wrote, "shows me much more than the ladies who are totally limited by conventional behavior. The working-class woman shows me her hands, her feet, and her hair. She lets me see the shape and form of her body through her clothes. She presents herself and the expression of her feelings openly, without disguises."[21]

Kollwitz had the sculptor's need to see people as objects, but as Martha Kearns has pointed out, she was also one of the first artists to see women as subjects too, as "physical, rather than sexual beings," to "reject the common timeworn image of women as physically passive, their bodies of interest only as sex objects or as objects of beauty," and to project "an unfamiliar affirmative view of working-class women, as persons of character and mental ability, fully responsive to the full range of human feeling."[22] In fact, it is impossible to discuss Kollwitz without including her feminism. She was truly a "woman-identified woman," synthesizing what we now categorize as socialist feminism and cultural feminism. (The latter is epitomized by an image from 1899 which shows a nude woman kneeling before a towering female god with arms outstretched, a fusion of Christ and the Mother Goddess.)

While she attributed her artistic success to the "masculine" side of herself rather than to a female strength, Kollwitz's female identity was strong enough to resist the conflict (as common now as then) between marriage and career, and to defy the notion (supported by her friends and fellow students at the Art School for Women in Berlin) that celibacy was the rule, since a woman artist's independence was as crucial as her talent. Kollwitz opted for marriage to a highly supportive man, and for bearing two children, and for making art as well. Her very courage in doing so probably went a long way toward insuring her success in all three roles. By the time she was thirty-two, she was a relatively famous artist. Yet she was also effectively isolated from her peers. She enjoyed the company of male artists

in her intimate circle, but she was far greater than any of them, and few of her independent women friends from art school seem to have survived as professionals.

In 1918 Kollwitz recognized this situation in a statement on the need to educate women artists on an equal basis with men: "I am in favor of permitting women to enter the State art academies, provided, however, that those admitted are carefully selected, so as not to further promote the widespread occurrence of substandard women's art."[23] Her feminism was apparent in her art in several direct and subtle ways. For instance, as Renate Hinz observes in this book, she always pictured the side of the battle she herself identified with, through "a kind of body language of the oppressed." The aggressors are always unseen. "In this indirect way, the dialectical relationship is expressed more clearly than it could be in direct confrontations." This is a peculiarly female kind of protest, rooted in the artist's longstanding sympathies with the women among whom she lived. Kollwitz managed to depict victims in a manner that endowed them with strength. Her maternal themes are also unlike those by men—many of which are not considered sentimental but are in fact far more so than hers. (Compare Michelangelo's *Pietà* with Kollwitz's squat, sculpted figure which quotes its source but portrays a grief far less rhetorical.) Any woman artist tackling the subjects closest to her gender roles—motherhood, eroticism, or children—is open to accusations of sentimentality. But Kollwitz virtually never referred to motherhood without also suggesting her other major themes: "herself; . . . the life of the proletariat; death as a force, and war."[24]

Kollwitz's views on war, and her pacifism, were embedded in her motherhood. After the death of a son and a grandson, her last lithograph protested the 1942 bombings and showed a hefty mother figure protecting a group of teenage boys from volunteering for the army. "Every war already carries within it the war which will answer it," she wrote pessimistically. "Every war is answered by a new war, until everything is smashed. That is why I am so wholeheartedly for a radical end to this madness and why my only hope is in world socialism. You know what my conception of that is and what I consider the only prerequisites for it. Pacifism simply is not a matter of calm looking on; it is work, hard work."[25] Just before her death she told her granddaughter, "One day, a new idea will arise and there will be an end to all wars. I die convinced of this. It will need much hard work, but it will be achieved."[26]

Kollwitz also recognized the connections between birth and creativity, not as a stereotype but as a biological fact of life to which women are more obviously attuned than men. When the birth of her second child came in the midst of her ambitious sequence *A Weavers' Rebellion,* she wrote in her diary that despite the added demands on her time and energy, "I was more productive because I was more sensual; I lived as a human being must live, passionately interested in everything."[27] At the same time, as Linda Nochlin has pointed out, Kollwitz always underplayed the "instinctual" aspects of the motherhood theme and placed her subjects "firmly into the bitterly concrete context of class and history." In works like the 1897 etching *Poverty,* she "set forth the material circumstances that prevent the working-class mother from fulfilling this natural destiny [feeding her child], thereby transforming her into the very personification of the proletarian victim of history."[28] Her success at making these connections is clear from the Nazis' rejection of her art, despite their romanticization of motherhood—outside any context except that of producing cannon fodder.[29]

Because of our dichotomous culture, there have been some curious views on Kollwitz's "maternalism." Baskin, whose own work has been influenced by Kollwitz's, called her self-portraits "the awful embodiment of maternal loss and suffering. . . . Kollwitz becomes more and more a mother-image in reverse."[30] Elizabeth R. Curry, also writing about the self-portraits, perceived this "reversal" as part of the same whole, but attached it to the linear progression of the artist's life. She saw a war with *age* at the core of Kollwitz's later vision; "and that war, frankly, is the secret of her ersatz 'motherhood' and 'mother and child themes.' Like the parent, the creative artist battles death by calling new life into being. . . . For woman, this discovery allows the female to be transcendent too, not merely earthbound, but also a being with a human—and therefore real— destiny."[31]

While this is an interesting idea, I suspect that the real burden Kollwitz was always trying to express was the burden of caring too much, the almost tragic concern of a person who cannot ignore what happens around her, to whom social justice is as necessary as food and shelter. She wrote of "the woman who feels everything" and said: "I want to do a drawing of a person who sees the suffering of the world."[32] She was, of course, that person herself; she did some one hundred drawings of her own weary face with the puffy eyes, sloping chin, and long upper lip, staring out sadly but fearlessly at an unsatisfactory world. It was in the human face and figure rather than in specific political events that Kollwitz saw the world reflected. When she viscerally internalized her subjects, it could affect her positively ("At such moments when I know I am working with an international society opposed to war, I am filled with a warm sense of contentment"[33]) or negatively ("While I drew and wept along with the terrified children I was drawing I really felt the burden I am bearing. I felt that I have no right to withdraw from the responsibility of being an advocate. . . . Work is supposed to relieve you. But is it any relief when in spite of my poster people in Vienna die of hunger every day? And

when I know that? Did I feel relieved when I made the prints on war and knew that the war would go on raging? Certainly not."[34]

Kollwitz often used herself as model for generalized Woman. She was capable of piercing and at times terrible insights into the relationship between self and society. She saw herself as the revolutionary Black Anna and the woman leading the rebellion in *Uprising* in the *Peasants' War,* as well as the mourning mother at her son's grave. The overused, misunderstood, but crucial feminist credo "the personal is political" takes on added resonance in Kollwitz's case. The contemporary artist Martha Rosler has shown how the personal *is* political when "one brings the consciousness of a larger collective struggle to bear on questions of personal life" and when "one is sensitive to the different situations of people within society with respect to taking control of their private lives."[35] Perhaps it is because Kollwitz was so successful at integrating these two significant elements of life that her work is so "unfamiliar" in these specialized times.

When Kollwitz was young, she saw herself in both the oppressed and the revolutionary woman. Her politics were unalterably affected by the death of her younger son during World War I. She found she could no longer maintain her "revolutionary hatred." Her pacifism led her to abandon communist sympathies for a more "moderate" position because she could no longer condone killing for any belief system. Disillusioned after the initial optimism of the Weimar period, she also questioned the whole romance of revolution:

In the meantime I have been through a revolution, and I am convinced that I am no revolutionist. My childhood dreams of dying on the barricades will hardly be fulfilled, because I should hardly mount a barricade now that I know what they are like in reality. And so I know now what an illusion I lived in for so many years. I thought I was a revolutionary and was only an evolutionary. Yes, sometimes I do not know whether I am a socialist at all, whether I am not rather a democrat instead. How good it is when reality tests you to the guts and pins you relentlessly to the very position you always thought, so long as you clung to your illusion, was unspeakably wrong. . . . [I] would probably have been capable of acting in a revolutionary manner if the real revolution had had the aspect we expected. But since its reality was highly unideal and full of earthly dross—as probably every revolution must be—we have had enough of it. But when an artist like Hauptmann comes along and shows us revolution transfigured by art, we again feel ourselves revolutionaries, again fall into the old deception.[36]

At the same time, the 1920s and '30s were Kollwitz's most activist period. She made some twenty posters and leaflets against those profiting from the postwar inflation that was causing so much misery, and against unjust abortion laws and their effect on working-class women; she worked with the Women's International League for Peace and Freedom and also supported the homosexual rights movement. Her memorial print to Karl Liebknecht, leader with Rosa Luxemburg of the Spartacus Party and assassinated with her in 1919, helped establish a fund for workers and artists in need. When Kollwitz was attacked by hardliners for making this work without being a communist herself (even though the subject was a family friend), she replied, "You can't expect an artist, who is moreover a woman, to find her way through all these insane, complicated circumstances. As an artist I have a right in every situation to extract the emotional component, to let it affect me, and to externalize it. Therefore I have the right to dedicate the work, without tacitly supporting Liebknecht politically." Then she added, "Or am I wrong?"[37]

Statements like these do not reflect a lack of commitment to the fundamental socialist ideals Kollwitz always held, but rather indicate her independence and her political honesty. Seven years later, when she made an official visit to Russia for the tenth anniversary of the revolution and exhibited her work in Moscow, she reiterated her position: "I am not a communist. But . . . as far as I am concerned, what has happened in Russia during the last ten years seems to be an event which both in stature and significance is comparable only with that of the great French Revolution."[38]

In 1931 Kollwitz's work was first published in China in the soon-to-be-banned magazine *Big Dipper,* where Lu Hsün saw it. He later recalled her 1923 print *The Sacrifice:* "a woodcut of mother with baby in outstretched arms."[39] Communist or not, Kollwitz was to be the most popular Western artist in revolutionary China, and her influence has survived the fall of the Cultural Revolution. In 1929 she was named in a German poll as one of three artists who best expressed the aspirations of the workers,[40] and her antiwar posters still turn up in demonstrations all over the world. Such affirmations from the masses must have mitigated the criticisms from left and right. Kollwitz had stated in the early 1920s her desire to "exert influence in these times when human beings are so perplexed and in need of help," and to "be the direct mediator between people and something they are not conscious of, something transcendent, primal." She succeeded then, and her art continues to succeed as an example for those who care enough about their art to want it to function in society.[41]

—*Lucy R. Lippard*

Notes

1. *The Diary and Letters of Käthe Kollwitz,* ed. Hans Kollwitz (Chicago: Henry Regnery Company, 1955), pp. 68–69.
2. This is partially accomplished from a feminist viewpoint by Martha Kearns's biography, *Käthe Kollwitz: Woman and Artist* (Old Westbury, N.Y.: The Feminist Press, 1976).
3. At the risk of doing my own dichotomizing, I would say the former attitude is more typically European and the latter more typically American.
4. *Eva Hesse* (New York: New York University Press, 1976).
5. Carl Zigrosser, *The Expressionists: A Survey of Their Graphic Art* (New York: George Braziller, 1957), p. 22.
6. Klinger, however, was a fantasist and his influence on Kollwitz can hardly be said to be stylistic, or anything more than an impetus to her own realism.
7. William S. Lieberman, in *German Art of the Twentieth Century,* ed. (New York: Museum of Modern Art, 1957), p. 188. This is the full Kollwitz entry.
8. Ulrich Weisner, *Käthe Kollwitz* (Bad Godesberg: Inter Nationes, 1967), p. 16.
9. Richard Huelsenbeck, quoting himself in his essay "Dada Forward" (1920), in Lucy R. Lippard, ed., *Dadas on Art* (Englewood Cliffs, N.J.: Prentice-Hall, Inc., 1971), p. 47.
10. Käthe Kollwitz, *Briefe der Freundschaft und Begegnungen* (Munich: List Verlag, 1966, p. 95, cited in Kearns, *Käthe Kollwitz.* p 172.
11. Francis Henry Taylor, exhibition brochure, n.d.
12. Leonard Baskin, *Massachusetts Review* 1, no. 1 (October 1959): 104.
13. Carl Zigrosser, *The Prints and Drawings of Käthe Kollwitz* (New York: Dover Publications, Inc., 1969), p. 19.
14. Kollwitz, *Briefe der Freundschaft.* p. 95, cited in Kearns, *Käthe Kollwitz.* p. 172.
15. Baskin, *Massachusetts Review.*
16. Kollwitz, *Diary and Letters.* p. 43.
17. Agnes Smedley, "Germany's Artist of the Masses," *Industrial Pioneers.* September 1925, pp. 8–13, cited in Kearns, *Käthe Kollwitz.* p. 82.
18. Kollwitz, *Diary and Letters.* p. 43.
19. Lise Kollwitz, *Monatsheft.* May 1917, cited in Kearns, *Käthe Kollwitz.* p. 148.
20. Muriel Rukeyser, "Käthe Kollwitz," in Kearns, *Käthe Kollwitz.* pp. 227–31.
21. Adolf Heilborn, *Die Zeidner des Volks I* (Berlin: Rembrandt Verlas, 1929), cited in Kearns, *Käthe Kollwitz.* p. 82.
22. Kearns, *Käthe Kollwitz.* p. 105.
23. Kollwitz, statement made in April 1918. This need to exclude ordinary women, and to be sure the women students were above average, is part

of a syndrome all too familiar to feminist artists today, but Kollwitz could not have known the ramifications of such statements then.

24. Kearns, *Käthe Kollwitz*, p. 155.

25. Kollwitz, *Diary and Letters*, pp. 183–84.

26. Otto Nagel, *The Drawings of Käthe Kollwitz* (New York: Crown Publishers, 1972), p. 94.

27. Kollwitz, *Diary and Letters*, p. 53.

28. Linda Nochlin, in *Women Artists: 1550–1950*, by Ann Sutherland Harris and Linda Nochlin (New York: Alfred A. Knopf, 1976), p. 67.

29. Actually, it was not her art but her politics that the Nazis rejected. They frequently published her work anonymously or under a fictitious male name, turning it into pro-Fascist propaganda.

30. Baskin, *Massachusetts Review*.

31. Elizabeth R. Curry, "Käthe Kollwitz: Role Model for the Older Woman," *Chrysalis* 7 (1979): 68.

32. Kollwitz, *Diary and Letters*, p. 97.

33. Kollwitz, *Diary and Letters*, p. 104.

34. Kollwitz, *Diary and Letters*, p. 96; when Kollwitz voted for the first time in January 1919, she voted for the moderates, but noted in her diary: "My feelings are more to the left."

35. Martha Rosler, speaking on a panel at the Institute of Contemporary Art, London, November 1980.

36. Kollwitz, *Diary and Letters*, p. 100.

37. Kollwitz, *Diary and Letters*, p. 98.

38. *Arbeiters International Zeitung* 20(1927), cited in Kearns, p. 194.

39. Lu Hsün, *New Republic*, May 28, 1945.

40. John Willett, *Art and Politics in the Weimar Period* (New York: Pantheon Books, 1978), p. 186. Grosz and Masereel were the other two most popular artists.

41. Käthe Kollwitz's work has been widely exhibited in recent years. Among the exhibitions in Germany were: *Käthe Kollwitz: Die Zeichnerin*, at the Kunstverein in Hamburg, November 8–December 28, 1980; *Käthe Kollwitz Frauen*, at the Neue Elefanten Press Galerie, Berlin, April 10–July 31, 1981; and *Dreimal Deutschland: Lembach, Lieberman, Kollwitz*, at the Kunsthalle, Hamburg, June 26–September 27, 1981. The Institute of Contemporary Arts in London is preparing a Kollwitz exhibition, together with the Kettleyard Gallery in Cambridge and the Scottish Gallery in Edinburgh. This exhibit, organized by Frank Whitford, will open in Cambridge before Christmas 1981, and in London in February 1982.

INTRODUCTION

A few years before her death in 1945, Käthe Kollwitz looked back on her career, sketching her development as an artist, commenting on the impulses that had inspired her work, explaining why it had always remained limited to certain themes, and responding to the attacks of some of her critics. The occasion for this retrospective self-examination was a questionnaire on the "dignity" of art, which had been sent to a hundred prominent artists in the years 1942 and 1943. The originator of this questionnaire had called Kollwitz's work "gutter art" and said she would have done better to become a union functionary. The only response of sufficient dignity to be worth mentioning occurs in Kollwitz's own reply. The political climate at the time of Kollwitz's remarks lends them the character of a manifesto; it is hard to imagine a document more appropriate to cite at the outset of this brief study.

Dear Sir: There have never been universally valid laws that prescribe what art should be. —The "common," the "obscene," the "repulsive" are not —to my knowledge —categories that have ever had a place in the definition of art, but the definition of what is common, obscene, repulsive has changed from period to period. Zola, for example, speaking as a representative of early Naturalism, coined the phrase: "Le beau c'est le laid." The artist is usually a child of his times, especially if his formative years fell in the period of early socialism. My formative years coincided with that period, and I was totally caught up in the socialist movement. At that time, the idea of a conscious commitment to serve the proletariat was the farthest thing from my mind. But what use to me were principles of beauty like those of the Greeks, for example, principles that I could not feel as my own and identify with? The simple fact of the matter was that I found the proletariat beautiful. I felt moved to portray the proletarian in his typical attitudes. It was not until later, when I came face to face with the poverty and misery of the workers, that I also felt the duty to put my art at their service. But it goes without saying that this is a far cry from tendentious art.

And here I have to say that you can't know my work very well if you label me an illustrator of the proletariat and nothing more. Over the decades, I kept extending the range of my work. I learned that, in addition to physical privation and misery, there was also a privation of the human soul, imposed by the laws of life. Separation, death are inevitable in every life. Goethe speaks of the "iron resonance of life." His image suggests all the basic experiences of a full life, without which there can be no life at all. One such basic experience is, for example, that of motherhood. After I had done a number of pictures of mothers and children, I said to myself: Now it is time to do what I call a definitive treatment of this theme. The result was my large sculpture of a mother and her two children. —I think you will have to grant that the range of my work is wider than you think, for you are not familiar with any of my sculpture. That is not surprising, because this work has not been exhibited for a long time now. But you should at least know my figures of a mother and father in the cemetery in Flanders. These brief remarks are my response to your questionnaire. I set no store by being numbered among the one hundred promi-

nent artists to whom you have sent it. . . . One final comment: I stand by every piece of work I have ever turned out. I meant every one to be as good as I could make it, which is to say, rigorous, never slipshod.

This statement contains a number of points that must be kept in mind in judging Kollwitz's work, and I want to review them briefly here:

Käthe Kollwitz did not object to interpretations that viewed her work from the perspective of economic and intellectual history. On the contrary, she encouraged such interpretation. Key terms like "early socialism," "Naturalism," "duty," and "tendentious art" suggest historical experiences of her lifetime, experiences that were incorporated into her work and that the critic has to attend to.

Her objection to the term "tendentious art" above has to be understood as an expression of her personal irritation with some of the undiscriminating criticism to which her work has been subjected. It is not meant as a wholesale rejection of partisanship in art. Indeed, it was Kollwitz herself who said, "It is all right with me that my work serves a purpose. I want to have an effect on my time";* and she made this declaration the basic postulate of her work. What her objection to this kind of art reveals in the quotation above is a fear that the subject matter she wanted to portray would forfeit its inner range and sense of wholeness if it were seen solely as an adjunct to current political statements.

"Sadness is a larger thing than social misery. It is life that contains everything within itself, and it is life that I am confronting in my work." This statement is the justified complaint of an artist who was always intent on uniting both the finite and the infinite, the fragment and the whole, in her aesthetic conceptions. She did not want her aesthetic productions seen simply as topical art or as political manifestos based on ethical imperatives. She wanted them to be regarded as objects of lasting value, which might well have been created for specific occasions (leaflets, posters, works commissioned for political uses) but which contained demands as yet unfulfilled, demands for a lasting peace and for truly humane living conditions for all people.

The sense of duty Kollwitz felt was to a large extent a legacy from her grandfather Julius Rupp, whose motto had been "Gabe ist eine Aufgabe," which can perhaps best be translated as "Talent is a responsibility," and this sense of duty also implied a commitment to technical perfection.

Numerous entries in her journal reflect her depressions and doubts, but they also record those rarer happy moments when she could feel how sensitive—yet at the same time strong— her artistic powers were: "I have never worked coolly but always, as it were, with my blood."

*This and all other unattributed quotations are taken from Kollwitz's diaries and letters.

At the same time that Kollwitz was exploring her themes, she was developing her formal techniques. In the graphic arts, she began with etching, turning to lithography and finally to woodcuts. After seeing proofs of her lithographs or etchings, Kollwitz did not hesitate to make changes and corrections in a printing plate that were as radical as those she might have made in a pencil drawing.

From the earliest stages of her career, Kollwitz's work and personality were shaped by two major factors: the intellectual atmosphere of her home and the physical environment of Königsberg, the East Prussian city where she was born and grew up. At home, the tone was set by her grandfather Julius Rupp (1809–1884), founder of the first Free Religious Congregation in Germany. This group rejected the authority of the state church and was committed to combining the ideals of early Christianity with the democratic impulses of the period. Kollwitz's father, Carl Schmidt, took over the leadership of the Free Religious Congregation after Rupp's death.

The Schmidt children, following their parents' lead, developed a keen interest in contemporary problems and issues. Kollwitz owed her schooling in socialistic thinking not only to her father but also to her older brother, Konrad (1863–1932), who later maintained a correspondence with Friedrich Engels and became the editor of the official Social Democratic Party (Sozialdemokratische Partei Deutschlands, or SPD) publication *Vorwärts*. Economics was as much a part of the Schmidts' intellectual fare as philosophy, literature, and history. They did not regard German classical literature, which is bourgeois in origin, and socialist theory as irreconcilable opposites but rather as related phenomena, both of which had valid exemplary characteristics. In this attitude, the Schmidts were fully in accord with the cultural policy of the Social Democratic Party at the time of Bismarck's anti-Socialist legislation.

Carl Schmidt had a lively interest in developing his children's talents. He was quick to encourage his daughter's artistic bent and provided her with academic training in art early on. Kollwitz took traditional lessons in drawing from the engraver Rudolf Mauer, who had her concentrate on drawing heads, working mainly from pictures and plaster casts. The eager student soon began enlivening and expanding this work with drawings from life, which she made on her walks through the streets and along the docks of Königsberg. She described being "powerfully" drawn to the type of motif that would later become a permanent part of her working repertoire: the dock workers loading and unloading sacks from the ships, and the Lithuanian and Russian boatmen dancing to accordion music on their barges in the evening.

What prompted Käthe Kollwitz to seize on these subjects was no childish whim but rather a strong and genuine interest in the life of working people, an interest she recognized early on. As she put it herself: "Motifs chosen from this sphere offered me, simply and directly, what I felt to be beautiful. . . . The largesse of movement in the working people was beautiful. People from middle-class life were completely without interest for me. Everything about bourgeois life struck me as pedantic. The movements of the proletariat were, by contrast, large and expansive."

Kollwitz's position, as revealed in this statement, was not that of an isolated rebel. If we consider the dominant styles in art in the 1870s and 1880s, ranging from the wax-museum realism of Anton Werner's school in Berlin to Makart's cult of beauty in Vienna, then Kollwitz's view appears almost to be the reaction we would expect from progressive middle-class intellectuals and from workers committed to the Social Democratic movement. During this period, Russian, Scandinavian, and French literature were the major sources of inspiration for art in Germany. Emile Zola, the major representative of Naturalism, had made the decline and fall of a Parisian working-class family the subject of his novel *L'Assommoir,* which appeared in 1877. This was the first serious portrayal of proletarian life in European art, and the first time subject matter of this kind had been incorporated into literature. The novel represented a convincing departure from the tenuous and empty image of humanity offered in fashionable art.

Käthe Kollwitz began formal art instruction in 1884 in Berlin with Karl Stauffer-Bern, who encouraged her in drawing and called her attention to Max Klinger's graphic work. She continued her studies in 1888–89 in Munich in Ludwig Herterich's painting classes. In the course of these years, she came to recognize that she had little talent for painting, and felt confirmed in this view after reading Klinger's *Malerei und Zeichnung (Painting and Drawing),* published in Leipzig in 1891. In this same year, external circumstances did their part to make painting of secondary interest in her career. She married Dr. Karl Kollwitz, who was just opening a practice in a working-class section of Berlin. She no doubt saw her decision to settle in Berlin and concentrate on graphic arts as a compromise solution that let her combine marriage and a career. She may have felt, too, that by making this decision she was at least partially following the advice her father had given her just before her marriage: "Be what you have chosen to be with all your heart."

Her first success as a graphic artist had come during her studies in Munich, and this was probably still a third factor affecting her decision. An association of student engravers to which she belonged had chosen the theme of *"Kampf"* (battle, struggle) as a subject; and her illustration, based on the scene in Zola's *Germinal* in which "two men in a smoke-filled pub fight over young Catherine," was much admired by her colleagues.

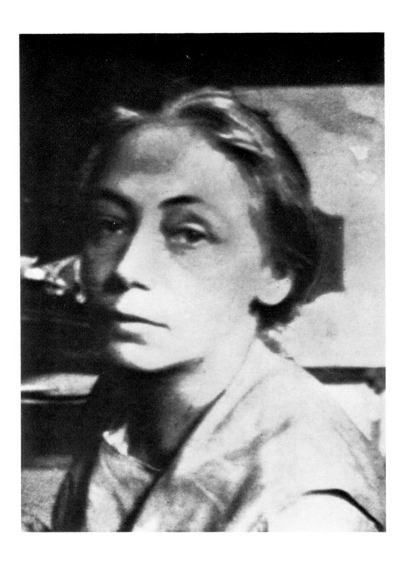

It was not pure coincidence that led Käthe Kollwitz to choose this subject. *Germinal,* which had appeared in 1885, had been a literary sensation. "All at once people began to see the same things everywhere: the misery of the proletariat, the degradation of the human being by modern wage slavery, and the gradual despoiling of the world caused by the spread of capitalism. . . . *Germinal* opened the eyes of all those who, up to this point, had not known what use to make of the revolutionary impulses they felt. Only now did they become aware of the soot-blackened, degrading aspect of the workers' quarters in their own cities. . . . Rasseneur's pub and the shooting galleries . . . were seen as genuine paradigms."[1]

In Munich during that same year, M. G. Conrad, an apostle of Zola's, founded the magazine *Die Gesellschaft (Society),* which became a forum for Zola enthusiasts.

The move from provincial Königsberg to the country's major city forced Kollwitz to break off her studies of the "characteristic situations" of working-class life that she had begun in Königsberg. She found the Berlin "working-class type" totally different from that in her home city. The Berlin type struck her as being "on a higher level," and she found that, given the way she perceived this type in "all its visible manifestations," she was "not able to make any artistic use" of it.

As a consequence, her early work in Berlin must be seen, first, as a testing ground for new graphic techniques but also — and more significantly — as a search for and exploration of new motifs, whose intellectual models Kollwitz took from contemporary Naturalism. Both in their dramatic light-and-dark effects and in their emphasis on the psychological, the genre-like illustrations *Four Men in a Pub* (Plate 8), *City Outskirts* (Plate 20), and *Young Couple* (Plate 25) show the influence of Edvard Munch, whose work was being shown in Berlin at the time.

Kollwitz's early self-portraits are the first in a long series that represent a continuing adjunct to her creative life. They can be seen as biographical soundings taken in the flow of historical experience and, in Werner Timm's phrase, as "psychograms of the world around her."[2]

Kollwitz recalled February 28, 1893, as a "milestone" in her career. This was the day when Gerhart Hauptmann's play *Die Weber (The Weavers)* was first performed in Berlin by the company *Freie Bühne.* Since the censors had not released the play for public viewing, it could be offered only in private performances; and the police were on hand at the premiere to enforce this ruling. The play focused on the misery of the exploited Silesian weavers after the brutal crushing of their rebellion in 1844. Competition from the industrialized textile mills was responsible for the disastrous living conditions of the hand weavers who worked out of their cottages. The mills offered their product at a considerably lower price than the weavers could afford. The middlemen, wanting to keep their profits up, paid less for handwoven goods, thus reducing the weavers' incomes below subsistence level.

The moral and political message of the play did not fall on deaf ears in the 1890s, when a wave of strikes was spreading rapidly throughout Germany. Walter Mehring has described the impact of *The Weavers* as that of a "sermon on the mount issuing from the Silesian Riesengebirge."[3] Kollwitz responded to the play with a cycle of six pictures (1893–98) called *A Weavers' Rebellion* (Plates 9–14). The two initial scenes, *Poverty* and *Death,* establish a mood of imminent revolt. *Conspiracy* — a reworking of previous pub scenes Kollwitz had done — captures the process of clarification and the emerging consciousness that provide the driving force of the drama. *The March of the Weavers* and *Riot* depict the uprising itself, which comes to its climax and its end in front of the ornamental wrought-iron gate of the factory owner's house. The motif of women and children in scenes of battle is one Kollwitz would use repeatedly in her portrayals of mass action. With it, she calls attention to the important role women play in social conflict and at the same time reflects views expressed by Bebel in his book *Die Frau in der Vergangenheit, Gegenwart und Zukunft (Woman in the Past, Present, and Future* [Zurich, 1883]). It is also characteristic of Kollwitz that the women she portrays are almost always mothers. Indeed, motherhood is a central motif in her work. The child is shown essentially as an attribute of the mother. Usually dependent on her, the child is drawn into the mother's immediate sphere of influence and shares in her fate.

Looking back on *A Weavers' Rebellion,* Kollwitz later recalled that another impulse behind the cycle had been the Old Testament principle of "an eye for an eye, a tooth for a tooth." This was the attitude that fueled the weavers' struggle, an attitude with which the artist fully identified. Unlike Hauptmann, Kollwitz conceived of her story solely from the perspective of the oppressed weavers, never wasting a glance on their opponents or making the slightest gesture toward impartiality. The existence of a political opponent is conveyed solely through the faces and gestures of the weavers. In this indirect way, the dialectical relationship is expressed more sharply than it could be in depicting a direct confrontation.

This body language of the oppressed became a characteristic feature of Kollwitz's art, and eventually took on exemplary significance. In accordance with this principle, she decided against using the symbolic etching *You Bleed from Many Wounds, O People,* 1896 (Plate 16), which she had planned as the concluding piece in this cycle. In its form and iconography, this picture is a relic of nineteenth-century bourgeois art that the artist had tried to press into the service of a social and political message. Kollwitz did, however, approve of and preserve the etching *The*

Downtrodden (Plate 15), which had originally formed the realistic, left-hand section of a larger etching by the same title. In this larger version of *The Downtrodden,* the right-hand panel had been *You Bleed from Many Wounds, O People.* She adheres to the symbolic formulation of motifs — a characteristic of contemporary art — whenever her motifs are drawn not from "a concrete social context but from the realm of the universally human."[4] Examples are her Pietà lithograph and her scenes involving death, woman, and child. By alluding to the Christian image of Mary weeping over the body of her dead son, Kollwitz, for the first time in her work, imparts to the idea of death a universal meaning that reflects the suffering of all humanity.

The numerous variations on the theme of death — represented in this volume by the etching *Death and Woman* (Plate 65) — also seem to reflect the artist's own maternal fears for the health of her children. By showing Death as a skeleton wrestling with a woman, Kollwitz makes use of a medieval pictorial concept that remained alive as an iconographical tradition well into the twentieth century. Death is shown as an enemy that wrenches life away from man. The confrontation with death is a central experience of life, which Kollwitz's work depicts in innumerable variations. The culmination of this theme is her late cycle entitled *Death* (Plates 123–130).

In the bourgeois art world, which was strongly opposed to the kind of art that enjoyed the patronage of the kaiser, Kollwitz's series of prints on the theme of *The Weavers* established her as a first-rate graphic artist. The first catalogue of her works was published in 1903, and public collections began buying her early prints. She had the further honor of winning the disapproval of the kaiser, who had once said, "Art should elevate and instruct. . . . It should not make the misery that exists appear even more miserable than it is." When the Weavers cycle was displayed in the Great Berlin Art Exhibit of 1898, the artists' jury, which included the painter Menzel, selected it for a gold medal, but the kaiser vetoed the award.

Kollwitz gradually overcame her initial uncertainty about her choice and formulation of motifs during the five years that she worked on the Weavers cycle. She drew on literary and historical themes for her work, showing a penchant for psychologically complex characters (such as Goethe's Gretchen) and dramatic ideas and situations.

In *La Carmagnole,* 1901 (Plates 23–24) — a work titled after a song widely sung during the French Revolution's Reign of Terror — Kollwitz shows men and women dancing frenetically around the guillotine, spurred on by the pounding of the drums. The dancers seem to be in an almost trancelike state that turns them into instruments of riot, murder, and chaos as they strike back at an oppressive social order. What is unique in this work is the detailed drawing of the massed buildings and the cobblestones. As the drawings and preliminary prints show, Kollwitz gradually worked her figures into this setting, showing these still unliberated dancers on their way toward liberation.

In *Uprising*, 1899 (Plate 29), a preliminary study for the Peasants' War series (1903–8), the psychological state of the rebelling peasants is symbolized by the allegorical figure of a Fury brandishing a torch. *Outbreak* (Plate 40), a work from the Peasants' War cycle, shows the peasants being spurred on by "Black Anna," a real figure drawn from Zimmermann's *Geschichte des grossen Deutschen Bauernkrieges* (*History of the Great German Peasants' War*), published in 1844. As in the Weavers series, Kollwitz lays the blame for the uprising on the peasants' catastrophic living and working conditions (*The Plowers* [Plates 31–32] and *Raped* [Plate 33]). But now Kollwitz goes a step further, focusing on the process by which the individual develops a consciousness of social conditions. The preliminary studies for *Whetting the Scythe* (Plate 36), which include the etching *Inspiration* (Plate 34), show the artist homing in on her theme. As she gives up the whole figure to concentrate on the head and upper body, she captures the psychological moment, the moment during the sharpening of the scythe when it suddenly occurs to the mower that she can use this tool as a weapon against inhuman working conditions.

And even though this plebeian uprising ended in defeat, it still remains clear that the "prisoners" of the final picture in the series are destined eventually to bring about the liberation of their class. That Kollwitz is not presenting merely historical material here but "the past infused with the present"[5] becomes evident in the *Help Russia* poster she did years later in 1921. She picks up the figure of a suffering young prisoner from the earlier work and transforms him into a symbol appealing for international aid to the young Soviet Union, whose people were threatened by war and famine.

The numerous studies Kollwitz did of working-class women from 1900 to 1910 demonstrate how intensely she worked to acquaint herself with the urban proletariat, to which she had at first felt she had no artistic access. Her 1910 portrait *Working-Class Woman (with Earring)* (Plate 61) brings to mind Karl Marx's observation that "the nobility of mankind shines out from faces hardened by labor." Through her husband's practice, Kollwitz soon gained considerable insight into "the profound struggle and tragedy of proletarian life." The harsh realities of working-class existence, such as prostitution and unemployment, troubled her so much that she felt she could make her own life bearable only by repeated efforts to portray proletarian life. Hence, the inscription on the drawing of *Frau Nitsche* (1904–5) contains no notes of an artistic nature but the name

and address of the model and information about her social condition: "Cleaning woman . . . without any other source of income, damp apartment."

From the early nineteenth century on, European poster art had used inscriptions to supplement the information provided by a picture. The confrontation with current problems in the working class and the resulting partisan position Kollwitz adopted obliged her to address an audience outside the fashionable art world. In the 1920s, she devoted more and more of her time to producing commissioned posters that, like Theophile Steinlen's illustrations, made a direct appeal for social change.

The element of social criticism was evident in Kollwitz's first poster, done for the German Home Industries Exhibit in 1906. It is hard to imagine a more striking pictorial indictment of the horrendous conditions prevailing in the cottage industries than this portrait of a careworn working woman. The piecework done in the home industries was scandalously underpaid. The men and women engaged in it worked excessively long hours under wretched physical conditions, without the guarantee of steady employment. On top of that, they were totally at the mercy of subcontractors who tried to reduce their wages even further. With her poster, Kollwitz once again incurred the displeasure of the kaiser's court. The empress refused to visit the exhibit unless the offending piece was removed.

In the years 1908 to 1911 Kollwitz's drawings appeared in *Simplicissimus*, a satirical weekly newspaper with a liberal political orientation. That *Simplicissimus* published her drawings for four years—works of social criticism that stood in sharp contrast to the satirical and humorous illustrations that dominated the weekly—attests to the reputation Kollwitz had attained. The terms under which she worked for *Simplicissimus* were the most ideal imaginable. The pay was good, and the choice of subject matter and style were left completely up to her. All the editors did was to add titles and captions. Kollwitz made fourteen drawings for *Simplicissimus* (Plates 46–59), all illustrating "the many sung and unsung tragedies of urban life." Eight of these drawings depict general aspects of the urban proletariat's social situation, e.g., widowhood, unemployment, hunger and despair, antisociality, unwanted pregnancy. The series *Scenes of Poverty* shows the "typical misfortunes of working-class families. If a man drinks or is sick or unemployed, the same things always happen. Either he is a dead weight on his family and lets them support him . . . or he kills himself. And the fate of the wife is always the same. She is left with children she has to support. . . ."

Unlike many contemporary illustrators of the urban environment, Kollwitz largely avoided any sentimental, pamphleteering elements. Her protest is truly effective because it "so convincingly links social comment to the reality depicted."[6]

Kollwitz's work for *Simplicissimus* forced her to conceptualize key themes quickly and to express them in a pictorial language that was accessible to a broad public. This brought about a major change in her mode of work. In the past she had carefully developed her pictorial ideas using live models, painstakingly working out every movement and detail. Now she shifted to a freer drafting style, dispensing with detail in order to focus on essential elements. The result was a compressed pictorial idiom that presented those elements almost as ciphers. Her earlier prints and drawings had either suggested or concretely depicted the worker's world. Now she focused exclusively on the human figure, using it alone to convey the social problems she envisioned. In this phase of her artistic development, she had such a large store of studies on hand and was so practiced in her draftsmanship that she could work without models.

The period 1910 to 1918 represents something of a hiatus in Kollwitz's graphic work. The main reason for this is the outbreak of World War I. Early in the war, her younger son Peter (1896–1914) was killed. His death struck "like a thunderbolt" and "crippled [her] work for a long time." But of at least equal significance was her sense that she had exhausted her possibilities as an engraver. She was beginning to sculpt now, and this new medium assumed more and more importance for her.

Despite all this, Kollwitz continued to do some graphic work, and she produced a number of documents that vividly capture this period. Her 1912 poster *For Greater Berlin* (Plate 67) evoked the wrath of the kaiser's censors and was banned because it "incited to class hatred." A member of the landlords' and real estate owners' association had lodged the complaint.

The figure of the undernourished girl, holding a little boy in her arms and standing in front of an apartment house doorway by a sign forbidding children to play in the courtyard, symbolizes all the inhuman conditions that must be endured by proletarian children. The scene speaks volumes about the power structure of a society that defends the interests of property owners, such as landlords, but leaves working-class families unprotected from the chicanery and high-handed decisions of the propertied class. *Run Over*, 1910 (Plate 66), shows the dangers that these children, forced to play in the streets, are exposed to.

March Cemetery, 1913 (Plate 68) commemorates the democratic revolution of 1848 in Berlin. Every year on March 18, the date on which the reactionary government violently crushed the revolution, the workers of Berlin paid their respects to the dead. "From morning till night, the workers' slow procession filed by the graves. . . ." Käthe Kollwitz, true to the legacy of her grandfather Rupp, always walked in these ranks.

The 1914 lithograph *Anxiety* or *Waiting* (Plate 69) and two others entitled *Widow* (1915–16) are Kollwitz's only public commentaries on World War I. *Anxiety* was published in a

weekly art paper that Paul Cassirer put out under the title of *Kriegszeit (Wartime)*. But unlike many other prominent artists of her time, such as Liebermann, Gaul, Barlach, and Meidner, Kollwitz refused to submit any more work to this basically conservative and nationalistic publication in which the pacifist position was expressed only rarely, and then in muted tones. It is indicative of her growing pacifist convictions that after the death of her son Peter, she did not offer the 1914 drawing *Street Singers* (Plate 70) to *Kriegszeit*. She had accompanied this drawing with the text "Make ready . . . make ready for eternity." These words were taken from a sailors' song that was often sung in Berlin courtyards during the war.

During this same period Kollwitz developed the idea of creating a memorial for her son. In 1932, her great antiwar monument, the two sculpted figures known as *The Parents* or *Mother and Father* (Plate 88), was placed in Roggevelde in Belgium. This sculpture is the most mature statement of an artist for whom war had been the great preceptor of pacifism.

The most productive phase in her career began in 1919. Inspired by Barlach, she began to work with the woodcut. She felt this was the medium in which she could give bolder expression to ideas she held with increasing conviction.

At the same time, a marked shift took place in the philosophical position underlying her work. The war had made a confirmed pacifist of Kollwitz. In the light of this new conviction, she gave up the revolutionary principle that condones battle as a means of altering social conditions. She became a great advocate for peace, and felt that her present political views were most in harmony with those of the "Majority Socialists." (When a radical SPD minority split off from the party in 1916 and formed the Independent Social Democratic Party, the larger number of Social Democrats remaining in the SPD constituted the Majority Socialists [*Mehrheitssozialisten*].) Although Kollwitz conceded during the November Revolution that the Spartacus League had the kind of political vigor that "might have prevented war," she still could not align herself with its aggressive actions and voted instead for the Majority Socialists," who believed in evolutionary change, i.e., in a "gradual transformation to socialism." Nevertheless, she was outraged at the base and shocking murders of the Spartacus leaders Rosa Luxemburg and Karl Liebknecht. Liebknecht's family asked her to do a portrait of the dead man. Her many preliminary drawings reveal deep personal feeling, shock, and sympathy. Among these studies is the 1919 drawing *Man and Woman* (Plate 75), which she made at the morgue where relatives of the many victims of the revolution came to view their dead.

In her memorial woodcut to Liebknecht, on the other hand, she felt she had achieved a highly differentiated aesthetic expression of the feelings she had in watching the workers pay tribute to their dead leader. "As an artist, I have the right to distill the emotional content out of everything and anything, to let that content take effect on me, and then to give outward expression to it. I also have the right to depict the workers' leave-taking from Liebknecht, indeed, the right to dedicate this work to the proletariat, without identifying myself with Liebknecht's political views. Or do I not? . . ."

Kollwitz became so involved in this theme that it took her two years after completing her initial drawing of Liebknecht's head to work through three different versions in different media: etching, lithograph, and woodcut. She regarded the last monumental formulation, cut in wood, as the definitive one. Following in the traditions of Jacques-Louis David, who "created, so to speak, the Pietà of the Revolution"[7] in his *Marat* (1793), Kollwitz links the dead leader of the working class, laid out on his bier, with salvation, although it is salvation in a purely political, rather than transcendental, sense. The caption under the picture reads "The Living to the Dead," a deliberate allusion to Freiligrath's poem "The Dead to the Living," which was dedicated to the victims of the Revolution of 1848.

Along with other progressive artists, Kollwitz had opposed the dominant trends in the art world under the kaiser. Her social convictions had motivated her stand against "pretentious studio art" in favor of "an art of reality." By this she meant an art that created "understanding between the artist and the people" and reestablished the "lost connection" between them.

With the Weimar Republic, the situation was different. The art world during this period was dominated by the conflict between bourgeois Modernism, which was now gaining acceptance, and the parallel development of proletarian and revolutionary art. Kollwitz, neither a cultural revolutionary nor a Modernist, spoke out against both these positions. "My art is not, of course, pure art in the sense that Schmitt-Rottluff's is, but it is art nonetheless. . . . It is all right with me that my work serves a purpose. I want to have an effect on my time, in which human beings are so confused and in need of help. Many feel the need to help and to be effective, but my way is clear and obvious. . . . Then there are all those groups that preach a new eroticism ('religious Bohemianism'). Our times are like the times of the Anabaptists, when, as now, a new age was proclaimed and the thousand-year Reich was said to be imminent."

True to her desire to have an effect on her time, she turned her work to the service of the workers' parties—the SPD and, on occasion, the Communist Party of Germany (Kommunistische Partei Deutschland, or KDP)—as well as the International Workers Aid (International Arbeiterhilfe, or IAH). She also contributed a number of illustrations to *Eulenspiegel*, a political and satirical magazine published by the KPD, and to the *Workers' Illustrated Newspaper (Arbeiter Illustrierte Zeitung,* or

AIZ). In addition, she did some sketches for bourgeois humanitarian organizations such as the Salvation Army, the Order of Good Templars, the Erfurt State Clinic for Women, and the Society for Social Reform.

Although there was much talk in the Weimar Republic about "peace, the rising standard of living, [and] organized capitalism,"[8] Kollwitz was quick to see the reverse side of the coin and to record what she saw in her *Three Leaflets against Profiteers*, 1920 (Plates 79–81); in her posters *Germany's Children are Starving!*, 1924 (Plate 98) and *Vienna Is Dying! Save Her Children!*, 1920 (Plate 78); in her 1924 lithograph *Bread!* (Plate 97), published in the IAH's portfolio *Hunger;* and in the series *Proletariat* (1925). In the latter series, the themes *Unemployed*, *Hunger*, and *Infant Mortality* were reworkings of problems she had already touched on in her earlier *Scenes of Poverty* (1909).

Kollwitz adopted an outspoken liberal position in support of other nations' right to peaceful self-betterment. She lent what aid she could to the newly founded Soviet Union with her 1921 lithograph *Help Russia* (Plates 83–84) and her 1923 woodcut *Hunger* (Plate 96), in which she reformulated the Christian Pietà motif as a universally applicable accusation.

The series *War*, 1922–23 (Plates 85–92), together with *Killed in Action*, 1921 (Plate 82), is a late echo of her own painful experience, which she would never fully put behind her. In *Volunteers*, the drummer leads a staggering corps to their deaths. The artist's own son Peter, whom she lost in the war, had likewise volunteered for military service.

She also made two posters on this same theme: *The Survivors — Make War on War!*, 1923 (Plate 93), commissioned by the Amsterdam International Association of Labor Unions for its antiwar day, and the lithograph *No More War* (Plate 102) for the Central German Youth Day in Leipzig. The upraised arm of the boy — a gesture that accompanies the swearing of an oath or an appeal to the masses in the French art — is meant as an explicit demand placed on society and humanity by the young. But Kollwitz herself must have felt how utopian was this transformation of Delacroix's boy with a weapon in his raised hand (*Freedom for the People* [1830]) into a proletarian youth making his appeal to humanity. "The demonstration 'No More War' was not a success. It was well attended. The youth organizations filled all the bleachers and looked very lovely and colorful, but what they had to say was pretty silly. It always strikes me as strange when masses of young people profess to be pacifists. I simply don't believe them. All it takes is one spark falling among them, and their pacifism is forgotten. The young working-class Communists are more honest. They want war and battle. The only difference is that they make war under different colors. Their standard is not black, white, and red but red alone."

Kollwitz's position as a well-known artist whose works were valued by bourgeois collectors as well as understood by the working class made it possible for her to take up this position beyond party lines. A number of her posters — without the lettering — were offered for sale on the art market. Part of the edition of her poster for the German Home Industries Exhibit in 1925, for example, was made available to the members of the German Art Society. Other posters that were printed without lettering and thus removed from the context of current political problems were: *Germany's Children are Starving!*; *The Survivors — Make War on War!*; *Bread!*; *Hunger*; *Karl Liebknecht Memorial*; *Mothers, Share Your Riches*; and *Help Russia*.

The idea of a pure socialism based on brotherly feeling, an idea to which Kollwitz remained true all her life, is not often represented in her work. There is but a hint of it in *Flags* (Plate 113), an image of flying "with the soles of one's feet turned upward,"[9] and in the cheerful portrayals of the positive aspects of proletarian life, such as *Working-Class Woman with Sleeping Child* (1927) and *Family*, 1928 (Plate 118). However, like many open-minded, liberal intellectuals, she followed the development of socialism in the Soviet Union with great interest. She had envied Maxim Gorky and his people for their faith in the "great, simple path" before them. She returned from her trip to Russia in 1927 with the lithograph *Listeners* (Plate 114). This work, like *Prisoners Listening to Music*, 1925 (Plate 109) and *Three Heads*, 1925 (Plate 110), no longer depicts the proletarian in suffering or violent rebellion, but shows instead a human being taking charge of his own fate and intent on catching up on the knowledge and culture of past centuries. That is Kollwitz's image of peaceful socialism.

In 1931, aware of the growing danger of fascism, the artist turned to the theme of demonstrations. The two versions we have of *Demonstration* (Plates 119–120) represent her most convincing rendering of the political power of the working people. To the issue of *Demonstration* that appeared in a supplement to the *AIZ*, she added in her own hand an inscription from Karl Marx: "We have a world to win."

Solidarity: The Propeller Song (Plate 121) was done in 1931–32 and was presented by antifascist groups to the Soviet Union in celebration of the fifteenth year of its existence. These groups saw support for the first socialist state as an increasingly important means of fending off fascism at home.

In *Solidarity*, the bound prisoners from the Peasants' War cycle have become a human chain, a bulwark against inhumanity. Ironically, the fact that the political opponents of German fascism failed to defeat it can be attributed in part to the lack of unity among them. Even after the Nazis assumed power, Kollwitz, along with others of similar convictions, publicly articulated the demand implicitly expressed in *Solidarity*: the demand for a coalition of the Social Democrats and the Communists. She reacted to the established German fascist government—however much it tried to convey a sense of initiative and youth—with the prophetic cycle *Death* (Plates 123–130). The pictorial formulations in this cycle had already been anticipated in her great series of drawings *Parting and Death* (1924). Her use of the figure of Death as an enemy goes back to the popular medieval concept of the "dance of death." The converse of this, the idea of Death as a friend, is borrowed from A. Rethel's woodcut series *Another Dance of Death* (1848).

As early as 1918, Kollwitz had quoted Goethe's dictum "Seed corn must not be ground" in response to Richard Dehmel's appeal that all able-bodied men volunteer for military service. This idea is reflected for the first time in her work in *The Mothers*, 1922–23 (Plate 91). Her pacifist conviction found its last pictorial expression in *Seed Corn Must Not Be Ground*, 1942 (Plate 132). Here the mother, an old woman trying to shelter the young under her cloak, is reminiscent of medieval Madonnas of mercy. This was Kollwitz's last work.

But Käthe Kollwitz's "effect" on her time did not come to an end with her death. Her most striking prints and posters seem particularly appropriate in our time in the struggle against war and for peace, disarmament, and humanitarian principles.
—*Renate Hinz*

Notes

1. Richard Hamann and Jost Hermand, *Naturalismus*, Epochen deutscher Kultur von 1870 bis zur Gegenwort, vol. 2 (Munich: Nymphenburger Verlagshandlung, 1972), p. 22.

2. Otto Nagel, ed., *Käthe Kollwitz: Die Handzeichnungen*, rev. Werner Timm (Berlin: Henschelverlag Kunst und Gesellschaft, 1972), p. 20.

3. Walter Mehring, *Die verlorene Bibliothek: Autobiographie einer Kultur* (Düsseldorf: Claassen Verlag, 1978), p. 98.

4. Günter Feist, "Zur Methodik der Kollwitz-Forschung," in Gerhard Strauss, ed., *Anschauung und Deutung, Willy Kurth zum 80. Geburtstag*, Studien zur Architekter- und Kunstwissenschaft, vol. 2 (Berlin: Akademie-Verlag, 1964), p. 92.

5. Jürgen Habermas, "Bewusstmachende oder rettende Kritik: Die Aktualität Walter Benjamins," in *Zur Aktualität Walter Benjamins* (Frankfurt am Main: Suhrkamp Verlag, 1970), p. 189.

6. Hamann and Hermand, *Naturalismus*, p. 10.

7. Klaus Lankheit, *Jacques-Louis David: Der Tod Marats*, Werkmonographien zur Bildende Kunst in Reclams Universal-Bibliothek, no. 74 (Stuttgart: P. Reclam, 1962), p. 18.

8. Wolfgang Hütt, *Deutsche Malerei und Graphik im 20. Jahrhundert* (Berlin: Henschelverlag, 1969), p. 214.

9. Maxim Gorky was quoted by Käthe Kollwitz in a statement published in the *AIZ* after her return from the Soviet Union in 1927: "In an essay he wrote during the early days of the Soviet Republic, Gorky speaks of 'flying with the sole of one's feet turned upward.' I believe I can sense such flying in the stormwind inside Russia. For this flying, for the fervor of their beliefs, I have often envied the communists" (*Arbeiter Illustrierte Zeitung* 20 [1927]).

Abbreviations Used Frequently in the Chronology and Notes on the Plates

AIZ *Arbeiter Illustrierte Zeitung* (Workers' Illustrated Newspaper)

IAH International Arbeiterhilfe (International Workers' Aid)

KPD Kommunistische Partei Deutschlands (Communist Party of Germany)

SPD Sozialdemokratische Partei Deutschlands (Social Democratic Party of Germany

XRR Khudozhniki Russkoi Revolutsii (Artists of the Russian Revolution)

KÄTHE KOLLWITZ

GRAPHICS

POSTERS

DRAWINGS

1. *Self-Portrait*, 1891–92

2. *Greeting,* 1892

4

3. *Man with Flat Hat*, 1891

4. *Self-Portrait at Table,* 1893

6

5. *At the Church Wall*, 1893

6. *Pub in Königsberg,* 1890–91

7. *Scene from* Germinal, 1893

9

8. *Four Men in a Pub,* 1892–93

9. *A Weavers' Rebellion*, leaf 1: *Poverty*, 1897

10. *A Weavers' Rebellion*, leaf 2: *Death*, 1897

11. *A Weavers' Rebellion*, leaf 3: *Conspiracy*, 1898

12. *A Weavers' Rebellion*, leaf 4: *March of the Weavers*, 1897

13. *A Weavers' Rebellion*, leaf 5: *Riot*, 1897

14. *A Weavers' Rebellion*, leaf 6: *The End*, 1897

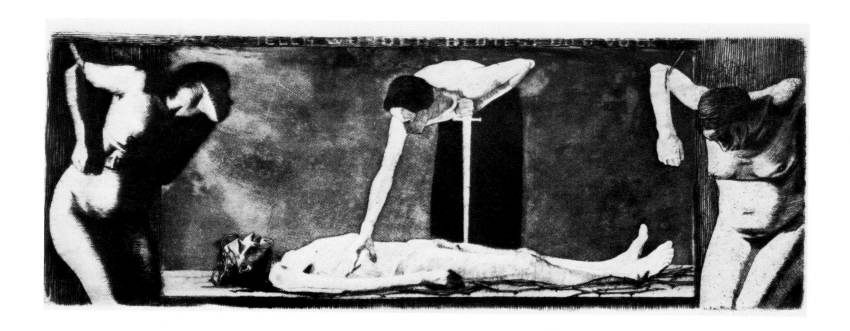

15. *The Downtrodden,* 1900
16. *You Bleed from Many Wounds, O People,* 1896

17

17. *Gretchen*, 1899, sketch for etching

18. *Gretchen*, 1899

19. *Woman with Folded Hands (Pregnant Woman)*, 1898

20. *City Outskirts*, 1901

21. *Hamburg Pub*, 1901

22

e, 1901

23. *La Carmagnole*, 1901, first state

24. *La Carmagnole*, 1901

25. *Young Couple*, 1904, second version

26. *Self-Portrait, Full Face, 1904*

27. *Half-Length Portrait of a Working-Class Woman with a Blue Shawl*, 1903

28. *Half-Length Portrait of a Woman with Folded Arms*, 1905

29

29. *Uprising*, 1899

30. *Plowers and Woman*, 1902, rejected lithograph for Peasants' War cycle

31. *Peasants' War*, leaf 1: *The Plowers*, 1906, first state

32

32. *Peasants' War*, leaf 1: *The Plowers*, 1906
33. *Peasants' War*, leaf 2: *Raped*, 1907

34. *Inspiration*, 1905, supplementary leaf to Peasants' War cycle
35. *Woman with a Scythe*, 1905, rejected leaf for Peasants' War cycle

36. *Peasants' War*, leaf 3: *Whetting the Scythe*, 1905

37. *Peasants' War*, leaf 4: *Seizing Arms*, 1906

38. *Three Rioters*, 1903, technical study for *Outbreak*

39. *Black Anna*, 1903, detail study for *Outbreak*

41. *Peasants' War*, leaf 6: *After the Battle*, 1907

42. *Peasants' War*, leaf 7: *The Prisoners*, 1908
43. *Bound Peasant*, 1908: detail study for *The Prisoners*

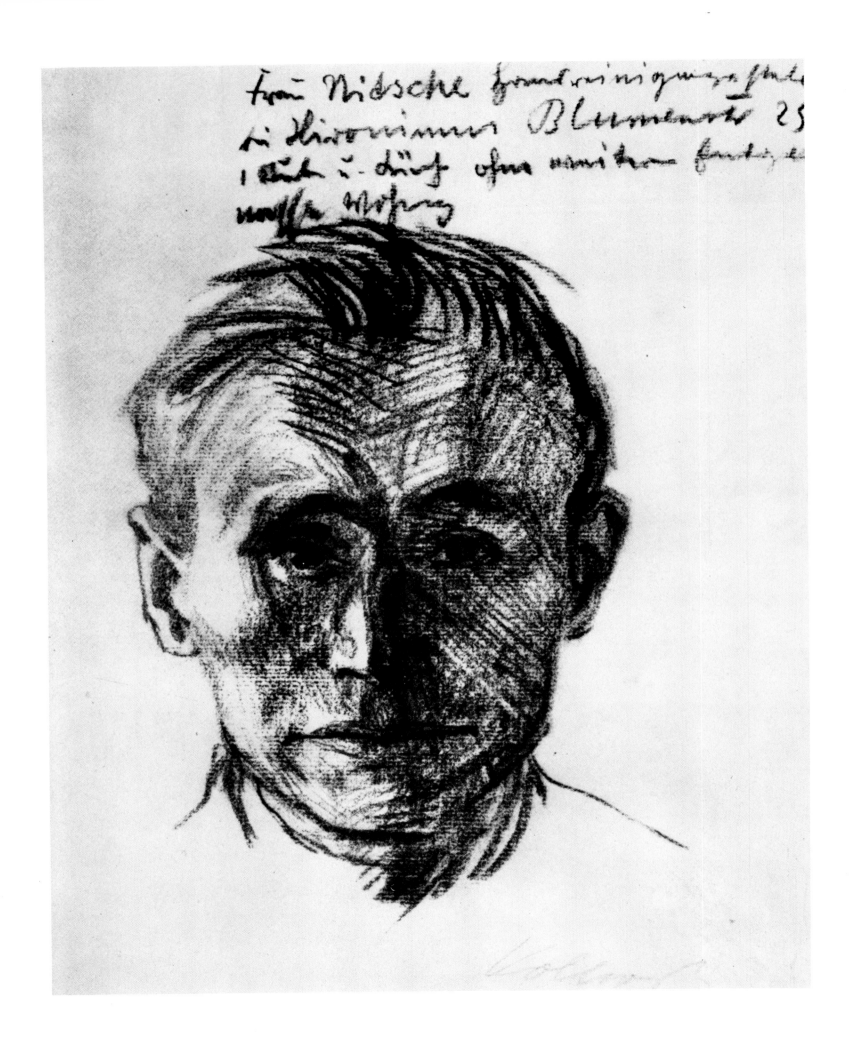

44. *Frau Nitsche*, 1904–1905

42

45. Poster *German Home Industries Exhibit 1906*, 1905

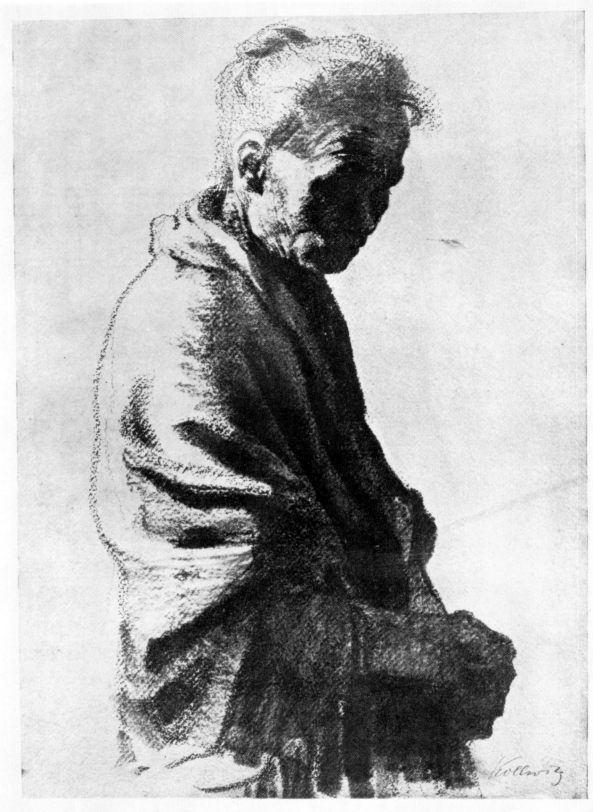

Mit Frömmigkeit grub man die Unfern ein;
Der liebe Gott mag zufrieden fein,
Ist alle Ehre ihm widerfahren
Von feinen Leuten, die dabei waren.
Sie wollten im Unglück, das uns geschehen,
Sein unerforschliches Walten fehen.

Fand auch der Paftor sich einen Spruch;
Die Bibel ift fo ein dickes Buch,
Daraus man feine Erbauung zieht,
Wenn armen Leuten recht weh gefchieht,
Der liebe Herrgott hat wohl getan;
So viele Reiche flehten ihn an

Und führten auf eine halbe Stunde
Den Allerbarmer in ihrem Munde.
Um diefe Ehre mochte er's wagen
Und konnte dreihundert Arme erfchlagen.

Ludwig Thoma

„Zehn Pennje her — ick bin die Portiersfrau von die Bank!"

47. *Lodging for the Night*, 1909

45

„Ich will mei'm Mann nich gratulieren, er schläft so schön."

„Verflucht, is das 'ne Kälte! Man könnt' meinen, der liebe Gott wär' Aktionär von 'n Kohlenbergwerk."

49. *Suspicion*, 1908–1909

„Trösten Sie sich, so hat das Kind wenigstens nicht erfahren, daß es unehelich war."

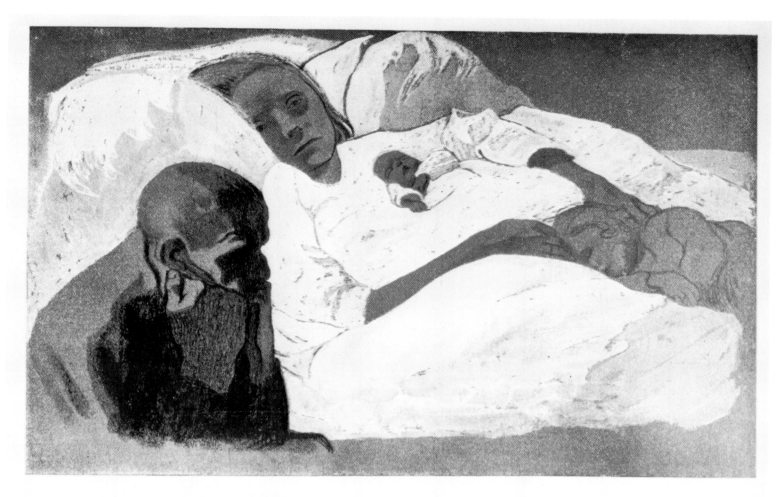

„Wenn sie nicht Soldaten brauchten, würden sie uns auch noch die Kinder versteuern."

„Mein' Bater feine Leich' hat 's Krankenhaus in die Anatomie g'schickt. Jetzt möcht' ich nur wiffen, ob fie das eiferne Kreuz auch in Spiritus gefetzt haben."

52. *The Cult of Military Honor in Baden*, 1909–10

„Arbeit kriegt man keine — und zum Stehlen sind die Hände zu schwielig."

53. *At the End*, 1909

54. *Scenes of Poverty*, leaf 1: *Home Industry*, 1909

55. *Scenes of Poverty*, leaf 2: *Pub*, 1908–1909

56. *Scenes of Poverty*, leaf 3: *At the Doctor's*, 1908–1909

57. *Scenes of Poverty*, leaf 4: *Suicide by Drowning*, 1909

58. *Scenes of Poverty*, leaf 5: *Drunken Man*, 1908–1909

59. *Scenes of Poverty*, leaf 6: *Christmas*, 1909

60. *Coal Miners' Strike:* 1909–10, sketch for drawing

61. *Working-Class Woman (with Earring)*, 1910

62. *Mother With Child on Her Arm*, 1910

63. *Self-Portrait with Hand on Forehead,* 1910

64. *Pietà*, 1903

65. *Death and Woman*, 1910

„FÜR GROSS BERLIN"

Öffentliche Versammlung
am SONNTAG den 3. MÄRZ
12 Uhr NEUE WELT
HASENHEIDE

Was erwarten wir vom Zweckverband?

Redner:

Bernhard Dernburg,
Oberbürgermeister Dominicus,
Muthesius, Südekum M.d.R.

Eintritt frei

Zur Deckung der Unkosten:
Reservierte Plätze à 5 Mk.
schriftlich vom Büro des Ausschusses für Gross Berlin
Grunewald, Trabener Strasse 25.

600000 Gross-Berliner wohnen in Wohnungen in denen
jedes Zimmer mit 5 und mehr Personen besetzt ist.
Hunderttausende von Kindern sind ohne Spielplätze

68. *March Cemetery,* 1913, detail study for lithograph

Das Bangen

Die „Kriegszeit" erscheint wöchentlich einmal. — Sie enthält künstlerische Beiträge in Form von Original-Lithographien.

Das Heft kostet im Einzelverkauf 15 Pfennig; bei Zustellung ins Haus, in gerollten Sendungen durch die Post, 25 Pfennig. Vorausbestellung mehrerer Nummern, unter Einsendung des Betrags, nehmen alle Buchhandlungen oder, falls keine Buchhandlung am Platze, der Verlag entgegen. Auf Wunsch Feldpostbestellungen.

Um vielen Wünschen entsprechen zu können, wird die „Kriegszeit" auch auf echtes Bütten-Papier abgezogen.
In dieser Ausführung (Ausgabe B) kostet die Nummer 50 Pf., 60 Hr.

Sammelmappen mit Titelaufdruck und Leinenrücken werden zum Preise von Mark 1.25, mit imit. Lederrücken zum Preise von Mark 1.50 abgegeben.
Verlag Paul Cassirer, Berlin W 10, Viktoriastr. 35. Verantwortlicher Redakteur: Alfred Gold, Berlin-Halensee. Druck von H. S. Hermann, Berlin SW.

70. *Street Singers*, 1914

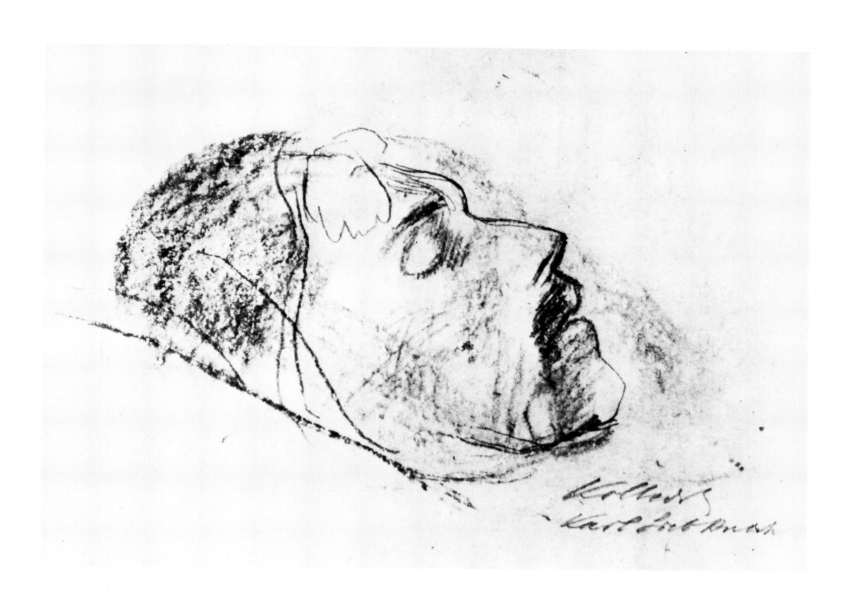

71. *Head of Karl Liebknecht on His Bier*, 1919

72. *Karl Liebknecht Memorial,* 1919, "Fragment"

73. *Karl Liebknecht Memorial*, 1920, preliminary drawing for woodcut

DIE LEBENDEN DEM TOTEN . ER

74. *Karl Liebknecht Memorial*, 1919–20

NERUNG AN DEN 15. JANUAR 1919

75. *Man and Woman*, 1919

76. *Self-Portrait*, 1919

77. Poster *Release Our Prisoners,* 1920

78. Poster *Vienna Is Dying! Save Her Children!*, 1920

Die Kranke und ihre Kinder.

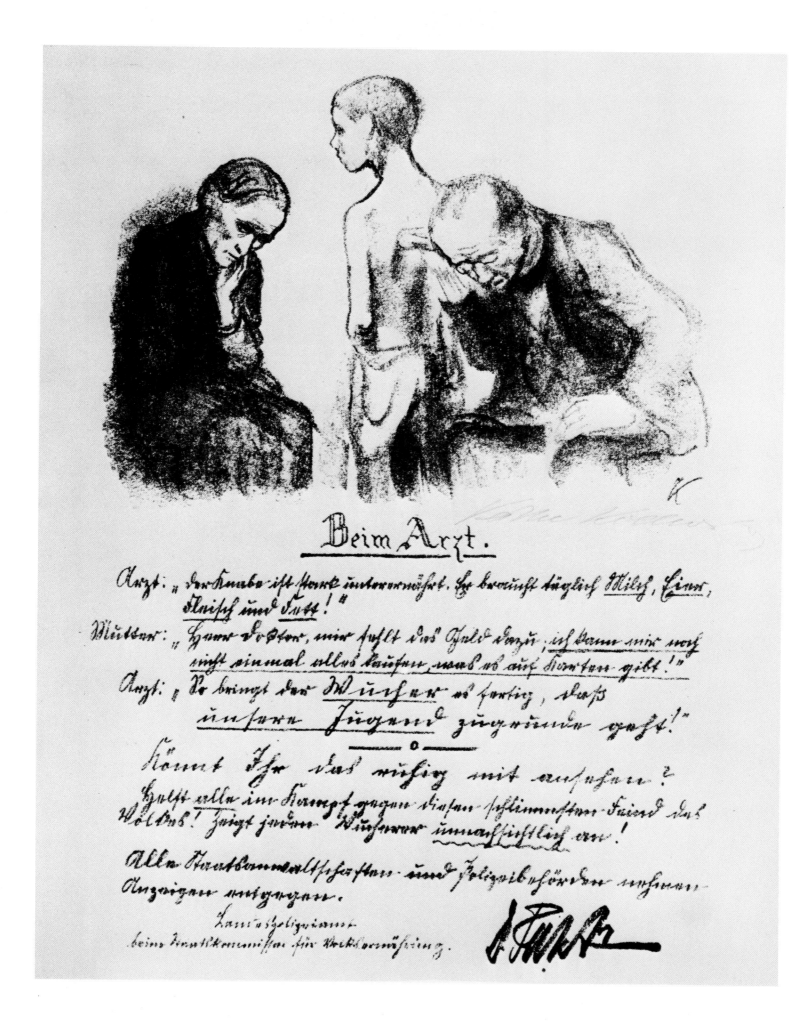

80. *Three Leaflets Against Profiteers*, leaf 3: *At the Doctor's*, 1920

82. *Killed in Action*, 1921, second version

83. *Help Russia*, 1921

84. Poster *Help Russia*, 1921

85. *War*, leaf 1: *The Sacrifice*, 1922–23

86. *The Volunteers,* 1922, sketch for woodcut

87. *War*, leaf 2: *The Volunteers*, 1922–23

88. *War,* leaf 3: *The Parents,* 1923

89. *War*, leaf 4: *The Widow I*, 1922–23
90. *War*, leaf 5: *The Widow II*, 1922–23

91. *War*, leaf 6: *The Mothers*, 1922–23

92. *War*, leaf 7: *The People*, 1922—23

93. Poster *The Survivors—Make War on War!*, 1923

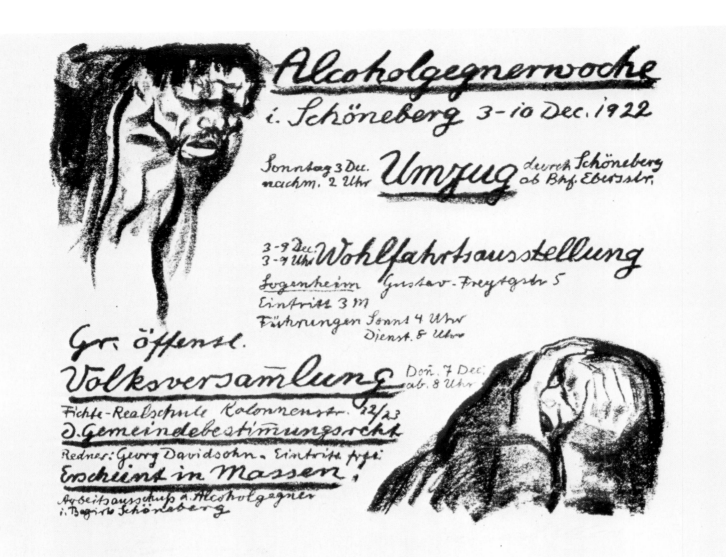

94. Poster *Temperance Week*, 1923

95. Poster *Down with the Abortion Paragraph!*, 1924

96. Leaflet *Hunger*, 1923

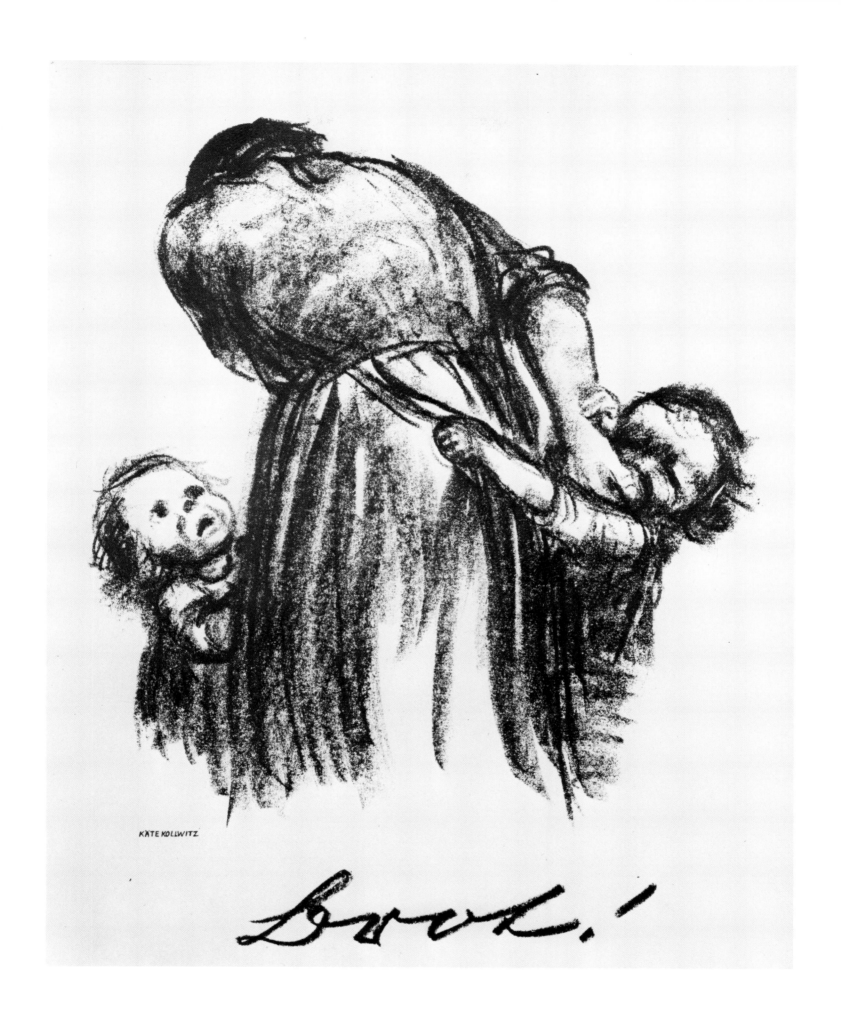

98. Poster *Germany's Children Are Starving!*, 1924

99. Poster *Our Children Are Starving!*, 1924

Wehrt dem Hunger!
Kauft Ernährungsgeld

Ernährungsgeld ist zu haben:

Bez. I Mitte
Wohlfahrtsamt, Stralauer Brücke 6, Zimmer 47.
Bez. I Tiergarten
1. Jugendamt, Dennewitzstr 24-a, Zimmer 2.
2. Wohlfahrtsauskunftsstelle, Kloppstockstrasse 24.
Bez. III Wedding
Auskunfts-u. Beratungsstelle des Wohlfahrtsamtes Wedding
Christianiastr. 13, Zimmer 14.
Bez. IV Prenzlauer-Berg
Frau Kenschke, Weissenburgerstr. 76.
Bez. I Friedrichshain
Wohlfahrtsamt Friedrichshain, Rigaerstr 102/103.
Bez. VI Kreuzberg.
Wohlfahrtsamt, Yorkstrasse 11-a, Zimmer 112.
Bez. VII Charlottenburg.
Jugendheim, Goethestrasse 22
Bez. VIII. Spandau.
Frau Köller, Bez.-Wohlfahrtsamt, Rathaus.
Bez. K Wilmersdorf.
Jugendamt, Wilhelmsaue 116/117.
Frl. Blumenthal.
Bez. X. Zehlendorf.
1. Frau Erdmann, Zehlendorf, Markgrafenstr. 1
2. Frau Wirth, Dahlem, Königin-Luisestr. 19.

Bez. XI Schöneberg.
1. Pestalozzi-Fröbelhaus, Schöneberg, Karl-Schraderstrß
Frl. X. von Gierke.
2. Frau Laskus, Friedenau, Wilhelmshöherstr. 2.
Bez. XII Steglitz.
Rathaus, Familienfürsorge
Lichterfelde, Rathaus, Familienfürsorge
Lankwitz, " " "
Bez. XII Tempelhof.
Wohlfahrtsamt, Mariendorf, Rathausstrasse 69.
Bez. XIV Neukölln.
Rathaus, Zimmer 272.
Bez. XV Treptow.
Frau Zobel, Treptow, am Park 44.
Bez. XVI Köpenick.
Rathaus, Zimmer 6, Frl. A. Magnus.
Bez. XVII Lichtenberg.
Stadthaus, Türschmidtstrasse 25., Dir. Krüger
Bez. XVIII Weißensee.
Wohlfahrtsamt, Wölkstrasse 1.
Bez. XX Pankow.
Wohlfahrtsamt, Rathaus, Zimmer 113, Fr. Dr. Eggeling.
Bez. XX Reinickendorf.
Wohlfahrtsamt, Hauptstr 46. Abt. Volksspeisung, Zim. 34.

100. Poster *Fight Hunger! Buy Food Coupons,* 1924

98

101. *Brotherly Feeling,* 1924

99

102. Poster *No More War*, 1924

103. *Death Swings His Lash over Mothers with Children*, 1922, sketch for *Hunger*

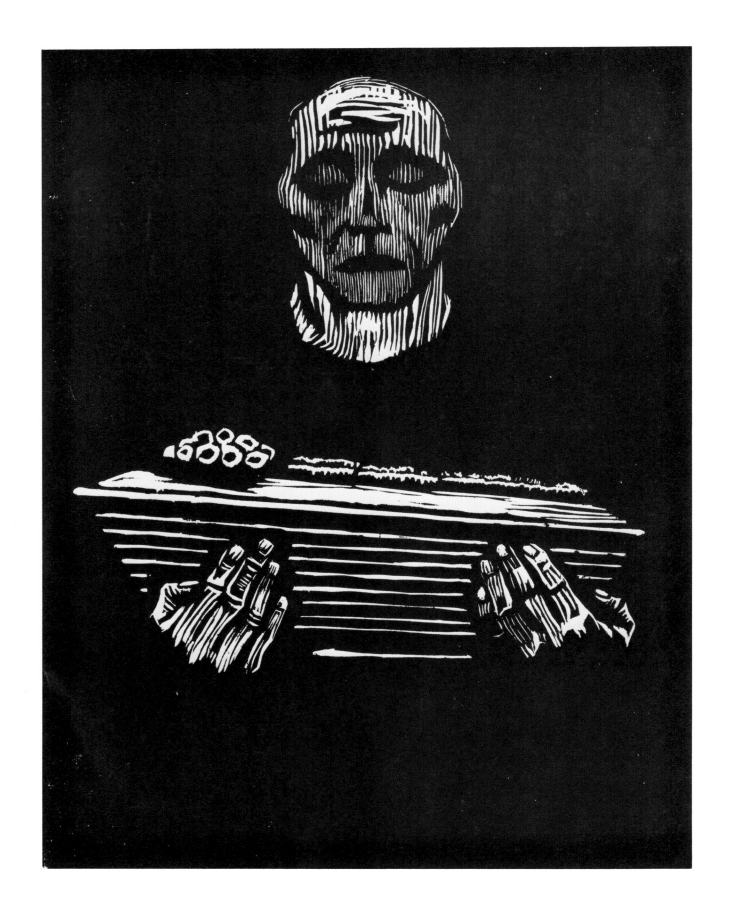

104. *Proletariat*, leaf 3: *Infant Mortality*, 1925

105. Poster *German Home Industries Exhibit 1925*, 1925

Arbeitende Frauen!

Nach dem Gesetz seid Ihr berechtigt,

6 Wochen vor der Niederkunft die Arbeit niederzulegen

Nach dem Gesetz dürft Ihr

6 Wochen nach der Niederkunft nicht beschäftigt werden

Bei Krankheit darf die Arbeitsruhe bis 12 Wochen nach der Niederkunft dauern

Während der gesetzlichen Arbeitsruhe darf Euch wegen Schwangerschaft und Niederkunft nicht gekündigt werden

Bei Niederlegung der Arbeit legt ärztliche Bescheinigung vor!

Mütter, stillt Eure Kinder!

Stillende Frauen haben während der Arbeitszeit Anrecht auf Stillpausen

Gesetz vom 16. Juli 1927 über die Beschäftigung vor und nach der Niederkunft. Die Bestimmungen gelten nicht für Hausangestellte, land- und forstwirtschaftliche Arbeiterinnen.

Bearbeitet im Kaiserin Auguste Victoria Haus, Reichsanstalt zur Bekämpfung der Säuglings- und Kleinkindersterblichkeit, Berlin-Charlottenburg 5, Frankstraße 3.

106. Poster *Working Women!*, 1925

107. *Standing Worker with Cap*, 1925

108. *Worker,* 1921–23

109. *Prisoners Listening to Music,* 1925

110. *Three Heads: Man, Woman, and Child*, 1925

111. Poster *Mothers, Share Your Riches!*, 1925

112. *Municipal Lodging,* 1926

113. *Flags*, 1925, preliminary drawing for *Song of the Revolution*

Zuhörende
in Moskau
(Feiern 1927)

Käthe Kollwitz

DAS NEUE RUSSLAND

ZEITSCHRIFT FÜR KULTUR, WIRTSCHAFT UND LITERATUR
HEFT 2 / 5. JAHRGANG / 1928 / PREIS: 0,80 MARK

114. *Listeners*, 1927

115. *Revolution*, 1928

116. Poster *Mother Krause's Happy Journey*, 1929

117. *Two Chatting Women with Two Children*, 1930

118. *Family*, 1928, sketch for lithograph

119. *Demonstration,* 1931, sketch for first state of the first version

120. *Demonstration,* 1931, second version

121. *Solidarity—The Propeller Song*, 1931–32

122. *Self-Portrait while Drawing, Left Profile,* 1933

123. *Death*, leaf 1: *Woman Giving Herself Up to Death*, 1934

124. *Death*, leaf 2: *Death Holding a Girl in His Lap*, 1934

125. *Death*, leaf 3: *Death Swoops Down on Children*, 1934

126. *Death*, leaf 4: *Death Seizes a Woman*, 1934

127. *Death*, leaf 5: *Death on a Roadside*, 1934

128. *Death*, leaf 6: *Death Recognized as a Friend*, 1934–35

129. *Death*, leaf 7: *Death By Water*, 1934–35

130. *Death*, leaf 8: *Death Calls*, 1934–35

131. *Self-Portrait*, 1934

132. *Seed Corn Must Not Be Ground*, 1942

CHRONOLOGY

1867   Born in Königsberg, East Prussia, on July 8, the fifth child of the master mason Carl Schmidt and his wife, Katharina (née Rupp).

1881–82   Takes art lessons in Königsberg with the painter G. Naujok and the engraver Rudolf Mauer.

1883   Meets Gerhart Hauptmann and Arno Holz in Berlin. Does a drawing illustrating Freiligrath's poem "Die Auswanderer" (The Emigrants).

1884–85   First trip to Munich. Studies with Karl Stauffer-Bern at the Art School for Women in Berlin. Her brother Konrad takes her to visit the "March Cemetery," which the victims of the street fighting in March during the Revolution of 1848 were buried. Becomes engaged to the medical student Karl Kollwitz, a Social Democrat and a friend of her brother Konrad.

1887   Receives art instruction from Emil Neide in Königsberg. His works *The World-Weary* and *At the Scene of the Crime* make a deep impression on her.

1888–89   Studies painting with Ludwig Herterich in Munich. In an etching club, recently formed by older students, she learns the techniques of the graphic arts. The works of Rubens that she sees in the Munich museum Alte Pinakothek make a lasting impression on her.

1890   Continues to work with etching under the tutelage of Rudolf Mauer in Königsberg.

1891   Marries Dr. Karl Kollwitz, June 13, and settles in Berlin.

1892   Birth of her first child, Hans, May 14.
Completes the etching *The Greeting*.

1893   Begins work on the cycle *A Weavers' Rebellion*.
Max Halbe's play *Jugend (Youth)* inspires her to do the print *Young Couple*.
At the Church Wall and other works shown in the open exhibit staged by the Association of the Eleven, a group formed after the jury of the Great Berlin Art Exhibit had refused to display the work of these eleven artists. The art critic Julius Elias calls attention to her work.

1896   Birth of her second child, Peter, February 6.

1898   Appointed to teaching position for etching and drawing at the Berlin Art School for Women, where Martin Brandenburg and Hans Baluschek also teach.
The Weavers cycle shown at the Great Berlin Art Exhibit. Kaiser William II vetoes the jury's award of a gold medal. First recognition for her work from a public institution: Max Lehrs, director of the Dresden Print Collection, buys her work. Joins the Berlin Secession, a newly founded organization opposed to the Great Berlin Art Exhibit.

1899   Awarded a gold medal at the German Art Exhibit in Dresden. Shows *Uprising* and other works in the Secession's first exhibit.

1900   Designs a cover for the program of the Berlin theater company *Freie Bühne*. This cover was used on all the company's programs from 1900 to 1914.

1902   The Berlin Print Collection buys her work. However, to avoid possible political embarrassment, the purchase is not made public.
Begins work on the Peasants' War cycle, completed in 1908.

1903   First catalogue of Kollwitz's work, compiled by Max Lehrs, published in the magazine *Die graphischen Künste (The Graphic Arts)*.

1904   The National Gallery in Berlin acquires five Kollwitz drawings. On the basis of her etching *Outbreak*, the Association for Historical Art commissions her to do a series on the Peasants' War. Studies in Paris. Makes first attempts at sculpture in classes at the Académie Julien.

1905   Designs poster for the German Home Industries Exhibit of 1906.

1907   Awarded the Villa Romana Prize, endowed by Max Klinger, which enables Kollwitz to make an extended stay in Florence as well as a side trip to Rome.

1908   The Peasants' War cycle is published.

1908–11   Contributes to the satirical weekly newspaper *Simplicissimus*, publishing a total of fourteen drawings in it.

1910   Begins working in sculpture.

1911–13   Sculpture *Lovers*.

1912   Designs the poster *For Greater Berlin* for the Committee for Greater Berlin, an organization devoted to developing comprehensive city planning for Greater Berlin.

1913   A catalogue of her etchings and lithographs, compiled by J. Sievers, is published by Emil Richter in Dresden. The magazine *Der Kunstwart* publishes a portfolio containing fifteen of Kollwitz's graphic works plus an introduction by Avenarius. Kollwitz's lithograph *March Cemetery* is used as a gift to subscribers of the *Freie Bühne* for the year 1913.

1914   Kollwitz's younger son, Peter, who had volunteered for military service, is killed in action in Flanders, October 22. On December 1, Kollwitz conceives the idea of creating a sculptural memorial to her son.

1917   Numerous exhibits of Kollwitz's work in honor of her fiftieth birthday. Paul Cassirer in Berlin, the Königsberg Art Association, the Bremen Art Museum, and the Berlin Secession all hold special exhibits.

1918   The socialist weekly paper *Vorwärts* publishes Kollwitz's response to Richard Dehmel's call to all able-bodied men to fight for the fatherland up to the very last day of war, October 18. Kollwitz counters this appeal by quoting Goethe: "Seed corn must not be ground."

1919   Kollwitz is appointed to the Prussian Academy of Arts and awarded a professorship, January 24. At the request of the Liebknecht family, does a drawing of the murdered political leader Karl Liebknecht, January 25.

1920   Retrospective show at the workers' exhibit on Petersburger Strasse in Berlin East. At this exhibit, a large unsigned edition of the woodcut *Karl Liebknecht Memorial* is offered for sale at a low price. Speaks at the burial of Max Klinger near Naumburg as a representative of the Free Secession. Designs posters appealing for aid in postwar emergencies: *Vienna Is Dying! Save Her Children!* and *Three Leaflets against Profiteers*. Makes a poster entitled *Release Our Prisoners* for the People's League for the Support of German Military and Civilian Prisoners.

1921   Supports the newly founded IAH and makes the poster *Help Russia* to recruit aid for the Volga River area in Russia, which had been struck by drought.

1922–23   The cycle *War* is published.

1924   Gerhart Hauptmann, *Abschied und Tod: Acht Zeichnungen von Käthe Kollwitz (Parting and Death. Eight Drawings by Käthe Kollwitz)* is published in Berlin. Does the poster *No More War* for the Leipzig SPD. For the IAH, makes the poster *Bread!*, which is published as part of the portfolio *Hunger*, and the poster *Germany's Children Are Starving!* Designs the poster *Down with the Abortion Paragraph!* for the Communist Party. Makes the lithograph *Brotherly Feeling* to be distributed with Henri Barbusse's book *Der singende Soldat (The Singing Soldier)*. The Artists' Aid Society uses the proceeds from the sale of her work in Wertheim's department store to support the IAH's campaign to feed the hungry.

1924–25   Several works included in the first German art exhibit to be shown in the USSR. The exhibit comprises 500 works and tours the cities of Moscow, Saratov, and Leningrad.

1925   Makes the lithograph *Three Heads: Man, Woman, and Child* as a supplementary leaf for the program at the *Freie Volksbühne* on Bülowplatz in Berlin. The Society for Social Reform commissions the poster *German Home Industries 1925* for a home industries exhibit it is holding in Berlin Alt-Moabit. Works on the woodcut series *Proletariat*.

1926   An exhibit including works by Kollwitz, Dix, Grosz, Nagel, Zille, Schlichter, and Sandkuhl is held in Berlin-Neukölln.

1927   Joins other artists, writers, and scholars in signing a public protest against the planned destruction of Heinrich Vogeler's Barkenhof frescoes. Numerous exhibitions are held honoring the artist on her sixtieth birthday, among them exhibits in the Berlin Academy of Arts and in the Berlin and Karlsruhe print collections. A wide range of lectures and articles are devoted to appreciations of her work. Shows in the exhibits *Woman in the Visual Arts*, *Kollwitz —Zille*, and *The Art of East Prussia*. On the invitation of the Association of Artists of Revolutionary Russia, she and her husband travel to the Soviet Union for the tenth anniversary of the October Revolution.

1928   Signs a protest against the construction of armored cruisers. Shows the lithograph *Municipal Lodging* in the "Porza" exhibit (Porza was an artists' association whose goal was to establish housing for artists in need of quiet surroundings where they could concentrate on their work). Designs the postcard *1918 + November 9 + 1928* for the Leipzig Social Democrats for the tenth anniversary of the November Revolution. Appointed to head the master studio for graphic arts at the Berlin Academy of Arts.

1929   Awarded the Prussian order *Pour le Mérite* for the arts and sciences. Designs the poster for *Mutter Krausens Fahrt ins Glück (Mother Krause's Happy Journey)*, a film in memory of Heinrich Zille. Kollwitz and Hans Baluschek head the sponsoring committee for the film. Major Kollwitz exhibit in Basel.

1931   Plaster figures of *The Parents* are shown at the spring exhibition of the Prussian Academy of Arts in Berlin.

Designs the lithograph *Demonstration* as a supplement to the May issue of the *AIZ*.

Kollwitz exhibit in Oslo.

Kollwitz's work appears in a Chinese publication for the first time: the magazine *The Great Bear* publishes *The Sacrifice* (from the cycle *War*).

1932   The figures of *The Parents* are exhibited in the National Gallery in Berlin. On July 30, they are placed in the military cemetery at Roggevelde in Flanders.

Exhibits in Moscow and Leningrad honor the artist on her sixty-fifth birthday.

Signs a poster urging the Communist Party and the Social Democrats to form a united front and present a joint list of candidates for the coming elections on July 31. Other signatories are Albert Einstein, Heinrich Mann, and Arnold Zweig.

Death of her brother, Konrad Schmidt, October 14.

1933   With her husband, signs an "urgent appeal" for the formation of a united workers' front and the coming together of the SPD and the KPD to fight German fascism. Under pressure from the Nazis, she and Heinrich Mann resign from the Prussian Academy of Arts, February 15. Relieved of her position as director of the master studio in graphic arts. Her husband is temporarily forbidden to continue his practice.

1934   Exhibits jointly with Nagel and Zille in Amsterdam, May.

1934–37   Works on *Death*, a series of eight lithographs. Five are shown in the November exhibit of the Berlin Academy. She discourages the attempt on the part of some friends to have her reinstated in the Academy. She prefers to remain among the "censured" and be an example for them.

1936   Unofficial ban on the exhibition of her work. Her original plaster for the figure of the mother in *The Parents* as well as her *Bronze Relief for a Family Grave* are removed from the Academy exhibit *Berlin Sculptors from Schlüter to the Present*.

Interrogated by the Gestapo because of an interview she gave the Soviet newspaper *Izvestia*.

1938   The National Socialists have her statute *Tower of the Mothers* removed from the exhibit in the studio building on Klosterstrasse.

1940   Death of Karl Kollwitz, July 19.

1941   Works on the lithograph *Seed Corn Must Not Be Ground*, December.

1942   Her grandson Peter is killed in Russia.

1943   Evacuation to Nordhausen. Air raid destroys many plates and prints in the Berlin apartment where she had lived for fifty years, November 23.

1944   Moves to Moritzburg near Dresden.

1945   Dies, April 22.

NOTES ON THE PLATES

Kl. = August Klipstein, *Käthe Kollwitz: Verzeichnis des graphischen Werkes* (Bern: Gutekunst & Klipstein, 1955).

T. = Otto Nagel, ed., *Käthe Kollwitz: Die Handzeichnungen*, rev. Werner Timm (Berlin: Henschelverlag Kunst und Gesellschaft, 1972).

The measurements given represent the height and width, respectively, of the picture in the case of prints, and the paper for drawings.

1. *Self-Portrait (Selbstbildnis)*, 1891–92. Pen and brush drawing in India ink, heightened with pastel chalks. 40 x 32 cm. T. 32.
2. *Greeting (Begrüssung)*, 1892. Etching. 11.8 x 8.8 cm. Kl. 10.
3. *Man with Flat Hat (Mann mit niedrigem Hut)*, 1891. Etching. 17.8 x 12.9 cm. Kl. 5.
4. *Self-Portrait at Table (Selbstbildnis am Tisch)*, 1893, second state. Etching and aquatint. 17.8 x 12.8 cm. Kl. 14.
5. *At the Church Wall (An der Kirchenmauer)*, 1893. Etching. 24.9 x 13.2 cm. Kl. 19.
6. *Pub in Königsberg (Königsberger Kneipe)*, 1890–91, preliminary study for *Germinal*. Pen in black India ink, brush in gray India ink on watercolor paper. 24.8 x 33 cm. T. 51.
7. *Scene from* Germinal *(Szene aus* Germinal*)*, 1893. Etching. 23.7 x 52.6 cm. Kl. 21.
8. *Four Men in a Pub (Vier Männer in der Kneipe)*, 1892–93. Etching. 12.9 x 15.9 cm. Kl. 12.

9–14. *A Weavers' Rebellion (Ein Weberaufstand)*, 1893–98
9. Leaf 1: *Poverty (Not)*, 1897. Lithograph. 15.4 x 15.3 cm. Kl. 34.
10. Leaf 2: *Death (Tod)*, 1897. Lithograph. 22.2 x 18.4 cm. Kl. 35.
11. Leaf 3: *Conspiracy (Beratung)*, 1898. Lithograph. 27.2 x 16.7 cm. Kl. 36.
12. Leaf 4: *March of the Weavers (Weberzug)*, 1897. Etching. 21.6 x 29.5 cm. Kl. 32.
13. Leaf 5: *Riot (Sturm)*, 1897. Etching and mezzotint. 23.7 x 29.5 cm. Kl. 33.
14. Leaf 6: *The End (Ende)*, 1897. Etching, aquatint, and mezzotint. 24.5 x 30.5 cm. Kl. 37.

15. *The Downtrodden (Zertretene)*, 1900, left-hand section of the etching *The Downtrodden*. Etching. 23 x 19.5 cm. Kl. 48.
16. *You Bleed from Many Wounds, O People (Aus vielen Wunden blutest du, oh Volk)*, 1896, rejected final leaf for the Weavers cycle. First version. Etching and aquatint. 12.9 x 33.3 cm. Kl. 29.
17. *Gretchen*, 1899, mirror-image sketch for the etching *Gretchen*. Brush with gray and black India ink and white highlighting on kreidegrundiert paper. 45.2 x 31.1 cm. T. 148.
18. *Gretchen*, 1899. Etching. 26.5 x 20.9 cm. Kl. 43.
19. *Woman with Folded Hands (Pregnant Woman) (Frau mit übereinandergelegten Händen [Schwangere])*, 1898. Etching. 28.6 x 22.8 cm. Kl. 41.
20. *City Outskirts (Vorstadt)*, 1901. Combination process with aluminum and copper plate, with hollowed-out places for the white areas. 22.8 x 17.9 cm. Kl. 54.
21. *Hamburg Pub (Hamburger Kneipe)*, 1901. Vernis mou. 19.2 x 24.7 cm. Kl. 58.
22. *Dance Around the Guillotine (Tanz um die Guillotine)*, 1901, preliminary mirror-image sketch for *La Carmagnole*. Pencil. 53 x 36 cm. T. 179.
23. *La Carmagnole (Die Carmagnole)*, 1901, first state. Etching and drawing. 57.3 x 34.3 cm. Kl. 49.
24. *La Carmagnole (Die Carmagnole)*, 1901. Etching, aquatint, and emery paper. 57.3 x 34.3 cm. Kl. 49.
25. *Young Couple (Junges Paar)*, 1904, second version. Etching. 29.7 x 31.8 cm. Kl. 73.

26. *Self-Portrait, Full Face (Selbstbildnis en face)*, 1904. Lithograph in three colors. 41.2 x 31.8 cm. Kl. 75.

27. *Half-Length Portrait of a Working-Class Woman with a Blue Shawl (Brustbild einer Arbeiterfrau mit blauem Tuch)*, 1903. Lithograph in three colors: light blue, dark blue, and brown. 35.2 x 24.6 cm. Kl. 68.

28. *Half-Length Portrait of a Woman with Folded Arms (Halbfigur einer Frau mit verschränkten Armen)*, 1905. Lithograph in two colors. 54.5 x 41 cm. Kl. 85.

29. *Uprising (Aufruhr)*, 1899. Etching. 29.5 x 31.7 cm. Kl. 44.

30–43. *Peasants' War (Bauernkrieg)*, 1902–1908

30. *Plowers and Woman (Pflugzieher und Weib)*, 1902, rejected lithograph for the Peasants' War cycle. Lithograph. 36.8 x 50.5 cm. Kl. 61.

31. Leaf 1: *The Plowers (Die Pflüger)*, 1906, first state. Etching and drawing. 31.4 x 45.3 cm. Kl. 94.

32. Leaf 1: *The Plowers (Die Pflüger)*, 1906. Etching and aquatint. 31.4 x 45.3 cm. Kl. 94.

33. Leaf 2: *Raped (Vergewaltigt)*, 1907. Etching and soft-ground. 30.8 × 52.8 cm. Kl. 97.

34. *Inspiration (Inspiration)*, 1905, supplementary leaf to the Peasants' War cycle. Etching and soft-ground. 56.4 x 29.7 cm. Kl 91.

35. *Woman with a Scythe (Frau mit Sense)*, 1905, rejected leaf for the Peasants' War cycle. Etching and aquatint. 36.7 x 19.8 cm. Kl. 89.

36. Leaf 3: *Whetting the Scythe (Beim Dengeln)*, 1905. Etching and soft-ground. 29.8 x 29.8 cm. Kl. 90.

37. Leaf 4: *Seizing Arms (Bewaffnung in einem Gewölbe)*, 1906. Etching and soft-ground. 49.7 x 32.9 cm. Kl. 95.

38. *Three Rioters (Drei Anstürmende)*, 1903, technical study for *Outbreak*. Etching. 14.8 x 14.8 cm. Kl. 64.

39. *Black Anna (Die schwarze Anna)*, 1903, detail study for *Outbreak*. Charcoal on grayish-yellow cardboard. 51.3 x 38 cm. T. 193.

40. Leaf 5: *Outbreak (Losbruch)*, 1903. Etching, pen-and-ink washout etching (Aussprengverfahren), textile texturing and aquatint. 50.7 x 59.2 cm. Kl. 66.

41. Leaf 6: *After the Battle (Schlachtfeld)*, 1907. Etching and soft-ground. 41.2 x 52.9 cm. Kl. 96.

42. Leaf 7: *The Prisoners (Die Gefangenen)*, 1908. Etching and soft-ground. 32.7 x 42.3 cm. Kl. 98.

43. *Bound Peasant (Gefesselter Bauer)*, 1908, detail study for *The Prisoners*. Charcoal. 50.8 x 43.8 cm. T. 431.

44. *Frau Nitsche*, 1904–1905. Black chalk on Ingres paper. 44 x 26.5 cm. T. 354.

45. Poster *German Home Industries Exhibit 1906 (Deutsche Heimarbeit-Ausstellung 1906)*, 1905. Lithograph. 69.2 x 48.5 cm. Kl. 93.

46. *Hamm*, 1908. Reproduction of the drawing *Standing Working-Class Woman (Stehende Arbeiterfrau)*, 1908 (T. 458), published in *Simplicissimus*, Vol. 13 (Nov. 30, 1908), p. 578.

47. *Lodging for the Night (Nachtasyl)*, 1909. Reproduction of the drawing *Julen*, 1909 (T. 487), published in *Simplicissimus*, Vol. 15 (Jan. 16, 1911), p. 721.

48. *New Year's Eve (Jahreswende)*, 1908. Reproduction of the drawing *Street Scene (Strasse)*, 1908 (T. 463), published in *Simplicissimus*, Vol. 13 (Dec. 28, 1908), p. 669.

49. *Suspicion (Misstrauen)*, 1908–1909. Reproduction of the drawing *Public Shelters (Wärmehallen)*, 1908–1909 (T. 469), published in *Simplicissimus*, Vol. 13 (March 1, 1909), p. 814.

50. *At the Deathbed of an Infant (Am Totenbett des Säuglings)*, 1908. Reproduction of the drawing *In the Childrens' Hospital (Im Kinderkrankenhaus)*, 1908 (T. 465), published in *Simplicissimus*, Vol. 14 (May 10, 1909), p. 89.

51. *The Only Good Thing About It (Das einzige Glück)*, 1909. Reproduction of the drawing *Unemployment (Arbeitslosigkeit)*, 1909 (T. 545), published in *Simplicissimus*, Vol. 14 (July 19, 1909), p. 267.

52. *The Cult of Military Honor in Baden (Veteranenkultus in Baden)*, 1909–10. Reproduction of the drawing *Petitioner (Bittstellerin)*, 1909 (T. 484), published in *Simplicissimus*, Vol. 14 (Oct. 11, 1909), p. 465.

53. *At the End (Am Ende)*, 1909. Reproduction of the drawing *Working-Class Family (Arbeiterfamilie)*, 1909 (T. 476), published in *Simplicissimus*, Vol. 15 (Oct. 10, 1910), p. 457,

54–59. *Scenes of Poverty (Bilder des Elends)*, 1908–1909

54. Leaf 1: *Home Industry (Heimarbeit)*, 1909. Reproduction of the drawing *Home Industry*, 1909 (T. 498), published in *Simplicissimus*, Vol. 14 (Nov. 1, 1909), p. 515.

55. Leaf 2: *Pub (Kneipe)*, 1908–1909. Reproduction of the drawing, 1908–1909 (T. 471), published in *Simplicissimus*, Vol. 14 (Nov. 15, 1909), p. 551.

56. Leaf 3: *At the Doctor's (Beim Arzt)*, 1908–1909. Reproduction of the drawing *At the Doctor's*, 1908–1909 (T. 475), published in *Simplicissimus*, Vol. 14 (Nov. 29, 1909), p. 587.

57. Leaf 4: *Suicide by Drowning (Ins Wasser)*, 1909. Reproduction of the drawing *Suicide by Drowning*, 1909 (T. 483), published in *Simplicissimus*, Vol. 14 (Dec. 20, 1909), p. 659.

58. Leaf 5: *Drunken Man (Betrunkener Mann)*, 1908–1909. Reproduction of the drawing *Drunken Man*, 1908–1909 (T. 475), published in *Simplicissimus*, Vol. 14 (Jan. 3, 1910), p. 695.

59. Leaf 6: *Christmas (Weihnacht)*, 1909. Reproduction of the drawing *Christmas*, 1909 (T. 502), published in *Simplicissimus*, Vol. 14 (Jan. 24, 1910), p. 747.

60. *Coal Miners' Strike (Kohlenstreik)*, 1909–10, sketch for the drawing *Coal Miners' Strike*. Pencil and charcoal on handlaid Ingres paper. 60 x 47.5 cm. T. 557.

61. *Working-Class Woman (with Earring), (Arbeiterfrau [mit dem Ohrring])*, 1910. Etching. 32.9 x 25.1 cm. Kl. 105.

62. *Mother with Child on Her Arm (Mutter mit dem Kind auf dem Arm)*, 1910. Etching. 26.7 × 21.9 cm. Kl. 110.

63. *Self-Portrait with Hand on Forehead (Selbstbildnis mit der Hand an der Stirn)*, 1910. Etching. 15.4 x 13.7 cm. Kl. 106.

64. *Pietà*, 1903. Lithograph. 45.3 x 61.3 cm. Kl. 70.

65. *Death and Woman (Tod und Frau)*, 1910. Etching and sandpaper aquatint. 44.7 x 44.6 cm. Kl. 103.

66. *Run Over (Überfahren)*, 1910. Vernis mou. 24.8 x 31.7 cm. Kl. 104.

67. Poster *For Greater Berlin (Für Gross Berlin)*, 1912, commissioned by the Committee for Greater Berlin. Lithograph. 70 x 90 cm. Kl. 119.

68. *March Cemetery (Märzfriedhof)*, 1913, detail study for the lithograph *March Cemetery*. Charcoal on handlaid Ingres paper. 32.9 x 28.2 cm. T. 713.

69. *Anxiety (Waiting) (Das Bangen [Das Warten])*, 1914. Reproduction of the lithograph *Waiting*, used as a cover for the weekly art publication *Kriegszeit*, No. 10 (Oct. 28, 1914). Kl. 126.

70. *Street Singers (Hofsänger)*, 1914. Crayon on white handlaid Ingres paper. 47.9 x 31 cm. T. 714.

71. *Head of Karl Liebknecht on His Bier (Kopf Karl Liebknechts auf dem Totenbett)*, 1919, study for the *Liebknecht Memorial*. Charcoal on heavy Japan paper. 27.8 x 41.4 cm. T. 767.

72. *Karl Liebknecht Memorial (Gedenkblatt für Karl Liebknecht)*, 1919, "fragment." Etching. 33.7 x 37.8 cm. Kl. 137.

73. *Karl Liebknecht Memorial*, 1920, preliminary drawing for woodcut. Brush and India ink on gray handlaid Fabriano paper. 34.5 x 50 cm. T. 781.

74. *Karl Liebknecht Memorial*, 1919–20. Woodcut. 35 x 50 cm. Kl. 139.

75. *Man and Woman (Mann und Frau)*, 1919, study at the morgue. Charcoal on gray-green cardboard. 39.9 x 29.7 cm. T. 798.

76. *Self-Portrait (Selbstbildnis)*, 1919. Lithograph. 34 x 29 cm. Kl. 133.

77. Poster *Release Our Prisoners (Heraus mit unseren Gefangenen)*, 1920, commissioned by the People's League for the Support of German Military and Civilian Prisoners. Lithograph. 67.8 x 91.7 cm. Kl. 142.

78. Poster *Vienna Is Dying! Save Her Children! (Wien stirbt! Rettet seine Kinder!)*, 1920. Lithograph. 92.5 x 56.5 cm. Kl. 143.

79–81. *Three Leaflets Against Profiteers (Drei Flugblätter gegen den Wucher)*, 1920, commissioned by the State Police Division assigned to the Commissioner of Public Nutrition.

79. Leaf 1: *Sick Woman and Her Children (Die Kranke und ihre Kinder)*, 1920. Lithograph. 17.5 x 28.5 cm. Kl. 148.

80. Leaf 3: *At the Doctor's (Beim Arzt)*, 1920. Lithograph. 19 x 25 cm. Kl. 150.

81. Leaf 2: *Waiting Room at the Pediatrician's (In der Sprechstunde des Kinderarztes)*, 1920. Lithograph. Kl. 149.

82. *Killed in Action (Gefallen)*, 1921, second version. Lithograph. 41 x 38.5 cm. Kl. 153.

83. *Help Russia (Helft Russland)*, 1921, without lettering. Lithograph. 40 x 47.5 cm. Kl. 154.

84. Poster *Help Russia (Helft Russland)*, 1921, commissioned by the IAH in Berlin. Lithograph. 66 x 47.5 cm. Kl. 154.

85–92. *War (Krieg)*, 1922–23.

85. Leaf 1: *The Sacrifice (Das Opfer)*, 1922–23. Woodcut. 37 x 40 cm. Kl. 177.

86. *The Volunteers (Die Freiwilligen)*, 1922, sketch for woodcut. Pencil on brownish handlaid Van Gelder Zonen paper. 47.4 x 66.5 cm. T. 849.

87. Leaf 2: *The Volunteers (Die Freiwilligen)*, 1922–23. Woodcut. 35 x 49 cm. Kl. 178.

88. Leaf 3: *The Parents (Die Eltern)*, 1923. Woodcut. 35 x 42 cm. Kl. 179.

89. Leaf 4: *The Widow I (Die Witwe I)*, 1922–23. Woodcut. 37 x 22 cm. Kl. 180.

90. Leaf 5: *The Widow II (Die Witwe II)*, 1922–23. Woodcut. 30.5 x 53 cm. Kl. 181.

91. Leaf 6: *The Mothers (Die Mütter)*, 1922–23. Woodcut. 34 x 40 cm. Kl. 182.

92. Leaf 7: *The People (Das Volk)*, 1922–23. Woodcut. 36 x 30 cm. Kl. 183.

93. Poster *The Survivors—Make War on War! (Die Überlebenden—Krieg dem Kriege!)*, 1923, commissioned by the International Association of Labor Unions, Amsterdam. Lithograph. 56.2 x 68.5 cm. Kl. 184.

94. Poster *Temperance Week (Alkoholgegnerwoche)*, 1923, commissioned by the German Order of Good Templars, Berlin-Schöneberg. Lithograph. 34 x 40 cm. Kl. 165.

95. Poster *Down with the Abortion Paragraph! (Nieder mit dem Abtreibungsparagraphen!)*, 1924, commissioned by the KPD. Lithograph. 47 x 43.5 cm. Kl. 189.

96. Leaflet *Hunger (Hunger)*, 1923, cover of the four-page leaflet published by Theodor Plievier, appealing for aid against famine in Russia. Woodcut. 49.7 x 35 cm. Kl. 169.

97. *Bread! (Brot!)*, 1924, commissioned by the IAH and published in the portfolio *Hunger. 7 Originallithographien . . . für die Internationale Arbeiterhilfe*. Berlin: Neuer Deutscher Verlag, 1924. Lithograph. 30 x 28 cm. Kl. 196.

98. Poster *Germany's Children Are Starving! (Deutschlands Kinder hungern!)*, 1924, commissioned by the IAH. Lithograph. 43 x 69 cm. Kl. 190.

99. Poster *Our Children Are Starving! (Unsere Kinder hungern!)*, 1924, for the Leipzig Winter Relief Fund. Lithograph. 43 x 29 cm. Kl. 190.

100. Poster *Fight Hunger! Buy Food Coupons (Wehrt dem Hunger! Kauft Ernährungsgeld)*, 1924. Lithograph. 35 x 44.5 cm. Kl. 193.

101. *Brotherly Feeling (Verbrüderung)*, 1924, supplement to Henri Barbusse, *Der singende Soldat*. [Mit Einleitung: Die logische Brüderlichkeit. Käthe Kollwitz schuf zu der Einleitung eine Originallithographie.] Leipzig: Verlag von Friedrich Dehne, 1924. Lithograph. 25.5 x 36.5 cm. Kl. 199.

102. Poster *No More War (Nie Wieder Krieg)*, 1924, commissioned by the Leipzig SPD. Lithograph. 94 x 70 cm. Kl. 200.

103. *Death Swings His Lash over Mothers with Children (Der Tod schwingt seine Geissel über Mütter mit Kindern)*, 1922, sketch for *Hunger*, leaf 2 of the cycle *Proletariat*. Brush and India ink. T. 954.

104. *Infant Mortality (Kindersterben)*, 1925, leaf 3 of the cycle *Proletariat*. Woodcut. 36.5 x 27.5 cm. Kl. 208.

105. Poster *German Home Industries Exhibit 1925 (Deutsche Heimarbeit Ausstellung 1925)*, 1925, commissioned by the Society for Social Reform. Lithograph. 34.3 x 42.7 cm. Kl. 209.

106. Poster *Working Women! (Arbeitende Frauen!)*, 1925, commissioned by the Reich Institute for Combating Infant and Child Mortality, Berlin. Reproduction of the lithograph *Mother Pressing Infant to Her Face (Mutter, Säugling an ihr Gesicht drückend)*. 26.5 x 27.5 cm. Kl. 214.

107. *Standing Worker with Cap (Stehender Arbeiter mit Mütze)*, 1925. Black chalk on yellowish, wood-fiber paper. 62.7 x 46.5 cm. T. 1102.

108. *Worker (Arbeiter)*, 1921–23. Charcoal on blue-gray Ingres paper. 45.8 x 56.8 cm. T. 921.

109. *Prisoners Listening to Music (Gefangene, Musik hörend)*, 1925, presented as a gift by the Kassel Art Association to its subscribers; also issued for other purposes. Lithograph. 56 x 40 cm. Kl. 203, IIa.

110. *Three Heads: Man, Woman, and Child (Drei Köpfe: Mann, Frau und Kind)*, 1925, supplement to the program of the theater *Freie Volksbühne* on Bülowplatz, Berlin. Lithograph. 12 x 15 cm. Kl. 210.

111. Poster *Mothers, Share Your Riches! (Mütter, gebt von eurem Überfluss!)*, 1925, commissioned by the Erfurt State Clinic for Women. Lithograph. 44 x 37 cm. Kl. 222.

112. *Municipal Lodging (Städtisches Obdach)*, 1926, presented as a gift by the Leipzig Art Association to its members; also issued for other purposes. Lithograph. 42 x 56 cm. Kl. 219.

113. *Flags (Fahnen)*, 1925, preliminary drawing for *Song of the Revolution (Revolutionsgesang)*. *Song of the Revolution* was reproduced as a cover for the songbook entitled *Deutscher Arbeiter-Sängerbund. Gemischte Chöre Alt. . . .* Berlin, 1926. Charcoal on handlaid Ingres paper. 46.5 x 60.3 cm. T. 1090.

114. *Listeners (Zuhörende)*, 1927. Reproduced as a cover for the magazine *Das neue Russland—Zeitschrift für Kultur, Wirtschaft und Literatur*, Vol. 5 (1928), No. 2. Lithograph. 22 x 19.3 cm. Kl. 228.

115. *Revolution (Revolution)*, 1928, sketch for a postcard, commissioned by the Leipzig SPD, in celebration of the tenth anniversary of the November Revolution. Charcoal and black chalk on yellowish handlaid Ingres paper. 60.5 x 46 cm. T. 1163.

116. Poster *Mother Krause's Happy Journey (Mutter Krausens Fahrt ins Glück)*, 1929, made for the film in memory of Heinrich Zille. Lithograph. Kl. 238.

117. *Two Chatting Women with Two Children (Zwei schwatzende Frauen mit zwei Kindern)*, 1930. Lithograph. 29.4 x 26 cm. Kl. 240.

118. *Family (Familie)*, 1928, sketch for the lithograph *Family* (1931) and *Maternal Happiness (Mutterglück)* (1931). Black chalk or charcoal. T. 1182.

119. *Demonstration (Demonstration)*, 1931, sketch for the first state of the first version. Reproduction of the lithograph in the *AIZ*. Charcoal on yellowish paper. 47.6 x 37.7 cm. T. 1200.

120. *Demonstration (Demonstration)*, 1931, second version. Lithograph. 36.9 x 26.2 cm. Kl. 242.

121. *Solidarity —The Propeller Song (Solidarität —Das Propellerlied)*, 1931–32. Lithograph. 56 x 83 cm. Kl. 248.

122. *Self-Portrait while Drawing, Left Profile (Selbstbildnis im Profil nach links, zeichnend)*, 1933. Charcoal on handlaid Ingres paper. 47.6 x 63.5 cm. T. 1240.

123–130. *Death (Tod)* (1934–35)

123. Leaf 1: *Woman Giving Herself Up to Death (Frau vertraut sich dem Tode an)*, 1934. Lithograph. 46 x 39.5 cm. Kl. 256.

124. Leaf 2: *Death Holding a Girl in His Lap (Tod hält Mädchen im Schoss)*, 1934. Lithograph. 43.4 x 37.8 cm. Kl. 257.

125. Leaf 3: *Death Swoops Down on Children (Tod greift in Kinderschar)*, 1934. Lithograph. 50 x 42 cm. Kl. 258.

126. Leaf 4: *Death Seizes a Woman (Tod packt eine Frau)*, 1934. Lithograph. 51 x 36.5 cm. Kl. 259.

127. Leaf 5: *Death on a Roadside (Tod auf der Landstrasse)*, 1934. Lithograph. 41 x 29.2 cm. Kl. 260.

128. Leaf 6: *Death Recognized as a Friend (Tod wird als Freund erkannt)*, 1934–35. Lithograph. 31.5 x 32.8 cm. Kl. 261.

129. Leaf 7: *Death By Water (Tod im Wasser)*, 1934–35. Lithograph. 48.5 x 38.4 cm. Kl. 262.

130. Leaf 8: *Death Calls (Ruf des Todes)*, 1934–35. Lithograph. 38 x 28.3 cm. Kl. 263.

131. *Self-Portrait (Selbstbildnis)*, 1934. Lithograph. 20.8 x 18.7 cm. Kl. 252.

132. *Seed Corn Must Not Be Ground (Saatfrüchte sollen nicht vermahlen werden)*, 1942. Lithograph. 37 x 39.5 cm. Kl. 267.

BIBLIOGRAPHY

No complete Kollwitz bibliography exists. Probably the best readily accessible bibliographies are those in Thieme and Becker, *Allgemeines Lexikon der bildenden Künstler* (1927) and in its continuation, Vollmer's *Allgemeines Lexikon der bildenden Künstler des XX. Jahrhunderts* (1956), which supply thorough listings of editions of the artist's works, of critical monographs and articles, and of exhibitions. This bibliography is intended to present a comprehensive listing of Käthe Kollwitz's *oeuvre* and a selection of secondary material published up to 1981. The various subdivisions of the bibliography—editions of her works, monographs, articles, exhibition catalogues, and catalogues raisonnés—are arranged chronologically in order to indicate the public reception of Kollwitz's art in different countries. Although the artist's major theme, the plight of the working classes, has established her as an artist of the proletariat in Eastern Europe and Russia, the bibliography does not adequately reflect her status in those countries because bibliographical access to their publications, especially to exhibition catalogues and dissertations, is difficult.

In general, items of only a few pages have been omitted from the bibliography, unless some special importance was felt to merit their inclusion. In particular, reviews and notices of exhibitions, as well as museum reports of new Kollwitz acquisitions, have also been omitted, as have most works in which Kollwitz is only one of several artists discussed.
—*Marion L. Buzzard, Adrienne R. Long*

Autobiography: Diaries and Letters

No complete edition of Kollwitz's diaries has ever been published.

Kollwitz, Käthe. *Tagebuchblätter 1909–1943 von Käthe Kollwitz.* 11 vols. (Manuscript diaries, located at the Akademie der Künste, West Berlin)

1948 Kollwitz, Käthe. *Tagebuchblätter und Briefe.* Edited by Hans Kollwitz. Berlin: Gebr. Mann Verlag, 1948.

1952 Kollwitz, Käthe. *"Ich will wirken in dieser Zeit." Auswahl aus den Tagebüchern und Briefen, aus Graphik, Zeichnungen und Plastik.* Edited by Hans Kollwitz. Berlin: Gebr. Mann Verlag, 1952.

1955 Kollwitz, Käthe. *The Diary and Letters of Kaethe Kollwitz.* Edited by Hans Kollwitz. Translated by Richard and Clara Winston. Chicago: Henry Regnery Co., 1955.

1957 Kollwitz, Käthe. *Aus meinem Leben.* Edited by Hans Kollwitz. List-Bücher, vol. 92. Munich: List, 1957.

1964 Kollwitz, Käthe. *Aus Tagebüchern und Briefen.* Selection by Horst Wandrey. Künstlerschriften. Berlin: Henschel-Verlag, 1964.

1966 Kollwitz, Käthe. *Briefe der Freundschaft und Begegnungen. Mit einem Anhang aus dem Tagebuch von Hans Kollwitz und Berichten über Käthe Kollwitz.* Munich: List, 1966.

1968 Kollwitz, Käthe. *Ich sah die Welt mit liebevollen Blicken. Ein Leben in Selbstzeugnissen.* Edited by Hans Kollwitz. Hannover: Fackelträger-Verlag, 1968.

Biography and Criticism: Monographs

1903 Lehrs, Max. *Käthe Kollwitz.* Die graphischen Künste, vol. 26. Vienna, 1903.

1907 Lüdecke, Heinz. *Käthe Kollwitz und die Akademie.* Berlin: Deutsche Akademie der Künste, 1907.

1908 Singer, Hans W. *Käthe Kollwitz.* Führer zur Kunst, vol. 15. Esslingen: Paul Neff Verlag (Max Schreiber), 1908.

1921 Kuhn, Alfred. *Käthe Kollwitz*. Graphiker der Gegenwart, vol. 6. Berlin: Verlag Neue Kunsthandlung, 1921.

1923 Kaemmerer, Ludwig. *Käthe Kollwitz; Griffelkunst und Weltanschauung. Ein kunstgeschichtlicher Beitrag zur Seelen- und Gesellschaftskunde*. Dresden: Emil Richter, 1923.

1924 Heilborn, Adolf. *Die Zeichner des Volkes: Käthe Kollwitz und Heinrich Zille*. Berlin-Zehlendorf: Rembrandt-Verlag, 1924.

1927 Diel, Louise. *Käthe Kollwitz; ein Ruf ertönt. Eine Einführung in das Lebenswerk der Künstlerin*. Berlin: Furche-Kunstverlag, c.1927.

1928 Diel, Louise. *Käthe Kollwitz; Mutter und Kind. Gestalten und Gesichte der Künstlerin*. Berlin: Furche-Kunstverlag, c.1928.

1945 *Käthe Kollwitz Feier in Moritzburg*. Dresden: Wilhelm Nestler, 1945. Independently published extract from *Volkzeitung* 37 (September 13, 1945).

1947 Fechter, Paul. *Käthe Kollwitz; Plastiken*. Berlin-Halensee: A. von der Becke, 1947.

1949 Heilborn, Adolf. *Käthe Kollwitz*. Die Zeichner des Volks, vol. 1. 4th rev. ed. Berlin: Konrad Lemmer, 1949.
Isenstein, Harald. *Käthe Kollwitz*. Copenhagen: J.H. Schultz, 1949. Also, Oslo: Dreyer, 1949.

1950 Strauss, Gerhard. *Käthe Kollwitz*. Künstlermonographien. Dresden: Sachsenverlag, 1950.

1951 Zigrosser, Carl. *Käthe Kollwitz*. Rev. ed. New York: George Braziller, 1951.

1954 Micheli, Mario de. *Käthe Kollwitz*. Arte Moderna Straniera, vol. 17. Milan: Hoepli, 1954.

1956 Schumann, Werner. *Käthe Kollwitz*. Das kleine Buch, vol. 1, 86. Gütersloh: Bertelsmann, 1956.

1958 Uhse, Bodo. *Die Aufgabe. Eine Kollwitz Erzählung. Zum 40. Jahrestag der Novemberrevolution*. Veröffentlichung der Deutschen Akademie der Künste. Dresden: Verlag der Kunst, 1958.

1961 Koerber, Lenka von. *Erlebtes mit Käthe Kollwitz*. Rev. ed. Darmstadt: Progress-Verlag, 1961.

1962 Klose-Greger, H. *Käthe Kollwitz; ein Lebensbild für die Jugend*. Berlin: Altberliner, Lucie Groszer, 1962.
Stopczyk, Stanislaw. *Kaethe Kollwitz*. Warsaw: Arkady, 1962.

1963 Bonus-Jeep, Beate. *Sechzig Jahre Freundschaft mit Käthe Kollwitz*. Rev. ed. Bremen: Karl Rauch Verlag, 1963.
Nagel, Otto. *Käthe Kollwitz*. Veröffentlichung der Deutschen Akademie der Künste zu Berlin. Dresden, Verlag der Kunst, 1963.

1964 Nündel, Harri. *Käthe Kollwitz*. Leipzig: Bibliographisches Institut, 1964.

1965 Nagel, Otto. *Die Selbstbildnisse der Käthe Kollwitz*. Berlin: Henschelverlag, 1965.
Schmalenbach, Fritz. *Käthe Kollwitz*. Die blauen Bücher. Königstein im Taunus: K.R. Langewiesche, 1965.

1967 Bauer, Arnold. *Käthe Kollwitz*. Berlin: Colloquium-Verlag, 1967.
Meckel, Christoph; Weisner, Ulrich; and Kollwitz, Hans. *Käthe Kollwitz*. Bad Godesberg: Inter Nationes, 1967. Essays and letters.
Porokova, S.A. *Kete Kol'vic*. Moscow: Molodaja Guardija, 1967.

1971 Nagel, Otto. *Käthe Kollwitz*. Greenwich, Conn.: New York Graphic Society, 1971.

1974 Timm, Werner. *Käthe Kollwitz*. Welt der Kunst. Berlin: Henschelverlag Kunst und Gesellschaft, 1974.

1975 Klein, Mina C., and Klein, H. Arthur. *Käthe Kollwitz; Life in Art*. Rev. ed. New York: Schocken Books, 1975.

1976 Kearns, Martha. *Kaethe Kollwitz; Woman and Artist*. Old Westbury, N.Y.: Feminist Press, 1976.

1977 Dobard, Raymond G. *Subject-matter in the Work of Käthe Kollwitz; an Investigation of Death Motifs in Relation to Traditional Iconographic Patterns*. Ann Arbor, Mich.: University Microfilms International, 1977.

Biography and Criticism: Periodical and Journal Articles

1901 Lehrs, Max. "Käthe Kollwitz." *Zukunft* 5 (1901): 351−55.

1902 Plehn, A.L. *Die Kunst* 5 (1902): 227−30. (Same as *Kunst für Alle* 17)

1903 Lehrs, Max. "Käthe Kollwitz." *Die graphischen Künste* 26 (1903): 55−67.

1904 Weisbach, Werner. *Zeitschrift für Bildende Kunst* N.F. 16 (1904−1905): 85−92.

1911 Jungnickel, M. *Die Aktion* 1 (1911): 587.

1912 Singer, Hans W. "Über die Zeichnungen von Käthe Kollwitz." *Mitteilungen aus den Sächsischen Kunstsammlungen* 3 (1912): 96−98.

1917 Avenarius. *Der Kunstwart* 30 (1917): 134−35.
Breuer, R. "Besprechung der Ausstellung Käthe Kollwitz in der Galerie Paul Cassirer." *Vorwärts* 34, no. 17 (April 29, 1917).
Elias, Julius. "Käthe Kollwitz." *Kunst und Künstler* 16 (1917): 540−49.
Kurth, Willy. "Käthe Kollwitz' Zeichnungen." *Kunstchronik* N.F. 28 (1917): 309−11.
Stern, Lisbeth, "Käthe Kollwitz." *Sozialistische Monatshefte* 23, part 2 (1917): 499ff. (Reprinted in Fritz Schmalenbach, *Neue Studien über Malerei des 19. und 20. Jahrhunderts*. Bern, 1955, pp. 36ff.)
Weinmayer, K. *Die Kunst* 35 (1917): 361−70. (Same as *Kunst für Alle* 32)

1921 Kaemmerer, L. *Jahrbuch der Originalgraphik* 3 (1921). Contains an original woodcut.

1925 Smedley, Agnes. "Käthe Kollwitz: Germany's Artist of the Masses." *Industrial Pioneers* 2 (September 1925): 8−13.

1926 Durus, Alfred. "Besprechung einer Ausstellung von Käthe Kollwitz." *Rote Fahne*, no. 231, 1926.

1927 Delphy, Egbert. "Käthe Kollwitz, zum 60. Geburtstag der Künstlerin." *Leipziger Neueste Nachrichten*, 1927.
Durus, Alfred. "Käthe Kollwitz zu ihrem heutigen 60. Geburtstag," *Rote Fahne*, no. 158, July 8, 1927.
Müller, J. "Käthe Kollwitz." *Allgemeines Lexikon der bildenden Künstler*, edited by Ulrich Thieme and Felix Becker. Leipzig: E.A. Seemann, 1927, pp. 21, 245−47.
Reifenberg, Benno. "Käthe Kollwitz." *Frankfurter Zeitung*, July 8, 1927.
Vonderbank, Karl. "Käthe Kollwitz, zum 60. Geburtstag." *Frankfurter Nachrichten*, July 9, 1927.

1929 Kühl-Classen, G. "Paula Modersohn und Käthe Kollwitz." *Die Schildgenossen* 9 (1929): 332–40.

1931 Worringer, Wilhelm. "Käthe Kollwitz." *Bilderhefte des deutschen Ostens* 10 (1931).

1937 McClausland, Elizabeth. "Käthe Kollwitz." *Parnassus* 9 (February 1937): 20–25.

1938 "German Art. Exhibition of Twentieth Century German Art at the New Burlington Galleries." *Apollo* 28 (1938): 94–95. Includes Barlach, Beckmann, Kollwitz.

1939 Devree, Howard. "Käthe Kollwitz." *Magazine of Art* 32 (September 1939): 512–17.
Kirkpatrick, D. "Artist of the People." *Design* 40 (March 1939): 16–18.

1945 Devree, Howard. "Friend of Humanity." *New York Times Magazine,* November 18, 1945, pp. 16–17.
Durus, Alfred, "Käthe Kollwitz," *Aufbau* 1 (1945): 225–29.

1947 Schreip, W. "Malerin und Plastikerin." *Bildende Kunst* 2 (1947): 4–7.

1949 Magritz, Kurt. "Käthe Kollwitz, eine Studie." *Bildende Kunst* 3 (1949): 271–75.

1953 Gurdus, L. "Käthe Kollwitz, Her Art Seen Through Her Self-portraits; Summary of Thesis." *Marsyas* 6 (1950–53): 85–86.
Oesterreich, Charlotte. "Umanità di Käthe Kollwitz." *Biennale di Venezia* 16 (1953): 11–14.

1955 Stika, Karel. "Grafická zbran Käthe Kollwitzové." *Hollar* 27 (1955): 20–24.
Tucholski, Herbert. "Vom Werden eines Werkes; über die Arbeitsweise Käthe Kollwitz." *Bildende Kunst,* 1955, pp. 101–107.

1956 "Käthe Kollwitz." *Allgemeines Lexikon der Bildenden Künstler des XX. Jahrhunderts.* Edited by Hans Vollmer. Leipzig: E.A. Seemann, 1956, vol. 3, pp. 90–91.

1957 Schmidt, Diether. "Symbolismus in der Kunst; über einen Vergleich zwischen Käthe Kollwitz und Pablo Picasso." *Bildende Kunst,* 1957, pp. 520–23.

1959 Süden, Richard. "Käthe Kollwitz und die Revolution." *Bildende Kunst,* 1959, pp. 98–102.

1960 Friedrich, Glaubrecht. "Käthe Kollwitz als Zeichnerin." *Dresdener Kunstblätter* 4 (1960): 148–50.

1961 Strauss, Gerhard, "Käthe Kollwitz." *Bildende Kunst,* 1961, pp. 89–97.
Zimmermann, Horst. "Gedanken zum Bildnis der Käthe Kollwitz von Leo von König." *Dresdener Kunstblätter* 5 (1961), 58–60.

1962 Sapego, I. "Nacalo puti." *Iskusstvo* 25 (1962), no. 11, pp. 53–61.
Stopczyk, Stanislaw. "An Early Drawing of Kaethe Kollwitz at the National Museum of Warsaw." *Bulletin du Musée National de Varsovie* 3 (1962): 125–28. Tavern scene, 1888.

1963 Feist, Günter. "Käthe Kollwitz; Weltanschauung und Künstlertum." *Bildende Kunst,* 1963, pp. 291–99.
Werner, Alfred. "The Art of Käthe Kollwitz." *American Artist* 27 (November 1963): 24–29, 57–59.

1964 Feist, Günter. "Zur Methodik der Kollwitz-Forschung," in *Anschauung und Deutung, Willy Kurth zum 80. Geburtstag.* Studien zur Architektur- und Kunstwissenschaft, vol. 2. Berlin: Akademic-Verlag, 1964, pp. 85–99.
Scharfe, Seigfried. "Käthe Kollwitz=religiös gesehen." *Pastoralblätter,* 1964.

1965 Rauhut, Ilse. "Die 'grosse Arbeit' gegen den Krieg." *Bildende Kunst,* 1965, pp. 186–90.

1966 Friedrich, Glaubrecht. "Hofsänger, eine neuerworbene Zeichnung von Käthe Kollwitz." *Jahrbuch der staatlichen Kunstsammlungen Dresden,* 1965–66, pp. 75–78.
Rauhut, Ilse. "Grab- und Gedenkmäler von Käthe Kollwitz." *Bildende Kunst,* 1966, pp. 70–86.
Raühut, Ilse. "Liebe und Verantwortung der Mütter; ein tragendes Thema im plastischen Werk von Käthe Kollwitz." *Bildende Kunst,* 1966, pp. 250–55.

1967 Abusch, Alexander. "Der Weg der Käthe Kollwitz." *Sinn und Form* 19 (1967): 1035–50.
Belogorlova, L. "Krov'iu serdtsa svoego." *Iskusstvo* 10 (1967): 63–71.
Feist, Peter H. "Käthe Kollwitz—eine grosse sozialistische Realistin." *Einheit* 22 (1967): 756–65.
Lüdecke, Heinz. "Unbekannte Werke von Käthe Kollwitz. Zum 100. Geburtstag der Künstlerin." *Bildende Kunst,* 1967, pp. 346–51.
Martschenko, Jelena. "Ich sah Russland im Lichte dieses Sterns." *Bildende Kunst,* 1967, pp. 595–99.
Reuschle, Frieda M. "Sie weiss um das Leid der Welt; zu Käthe Kollwitz' 100. Geburtstag." *Die Christengemeinschaft. Monatsschrift zur religiösen Erneuerung* (Stuttgart) 39 (1967): 182–85.
Robles, Hella. "Die graphischen Techniken der Käthe Kollwitz." *Museen in Köln Bulletin* 6 (1967): 582–84.
Schmidt, Werner. "Zur kunstlerischen Herkunft von Käthe Kollwitz." *Jahrbuch der staatlichen Kunstsammlungen Dresden,* 1967, pp. 83–90.
Sellgrad, Rolf. "Käthe Kollwitz." *Konstvännen,* 1967, no. 4, pp. 3–7; no. 5, pp. 3–5.
Whitford, Frank. "Käthe Kollwitz." *Studio International* 174 (167): 262–63.

1968 Andreeva, Violeta. "Kete Kolvic." *Iskusstvo* 18 (1968), no. 1, pp. 14–19.
Feist, Peter A. "Die Bedeutung der Arbeiterklasse für den Realismus der Käthe Kollwitz." *Wissenschaftliche Zeitschrift der Humboldt-Universität, Berlin. Gesellschafts- und sprachwissenschaftliche Reihe* 17 (1968): 705–25.
Förster, Ruth. "Die Wirkung von Käthe Kollwitz auf jüngere Künstler." *Wissenschaftliche Zeitschrift der Humboldt-Universität, Berlin. Gesellschafts- und sprachwissenschaftliche Reihe* 17 (1968): 727–40.
Gärtner, Hannelore. "Ein Werk gegen den Krieg für das Leben—Festvortrag anlässlich des 100. Geburtstages von Käthe Kollwitz." *Wissenschaftliche Zeitschrift der Ernst Moritz Arndt-Universität. Gesellschafts- und sprachwissenschaftliche Reihe* 17 (1968): 387–94.
Jansen, Elmer. "Zur Studienzeit Ernst Barlachs in Dresden. Mit einer Nachbemerkung zum Verhaltnis von Käthe Kollwitz und Ernst Barlach." *Wissenschaftliche Zeitschrift der Humboldt-Universität, Berlin. Gesellschafts- und sprachwissenschaftliche Reihe* 17 (1968): 749–58.

Matull, Wilhelm. "Was hat Königsberg Käthe Kollwitz mitgegeben?" *Jahrbuch der Albertus-Universtät zu Königsberg* 18 (1968): 232—47.

Schaumman. Wolfgang. "Zur 'grossen thematischen Komposition' bei Käthe Kollwitz." *Wissenschaftliche Zeitschrift der Ernst Moritz Arndt-Universität. Gesellschafts- und sprachwissenschaftliche Reihe* 17 (1968): 377—80.

Wittrin, Gabriele. "Die Einflüsse von Käthe Kollwitz auf die chinesische Graphik zwischen 1931 and 1949." *Wissenschaftliche Zeitschrift der Humboldt-Universität, Berlin. Gesellschafts- und sprachwissenschaftliche Reihe* 17 (1968): 741—47.

1969 Müller, Folkert. "Käthe Kollwitz und die sozialkritische Funktion der Kunst." *Theologische Zeitschrift* 25 (1969): 354—61.

Zinke, Erich. "Mein Besuch bei Käthe Kollwitz am 8, März 1942." *Dresdener Kunstblätter* 13 (1969): 179—82.

1970 Rudloff, Diether. "Ich soll das Leiden der Menschen aussprechen; zum 25. Todestag von Käthe Kollwitz." *Die Kommenden; eine unabhängige Zeitschrift fur geistige und soziale Erneuerung* 24 (1970): 11—13.

1971 Dreher, Eberhard. "Keine Untertanen: Heinrich Mann, Käthe Kollwitz, Martin Wagner." *Etudes Germaniques* 26 (1971): 344—48.

1972 Smith, R. "Käthe Kollwitz and the Nature of Tragic Art." *Art and Australia* 9 (March 1972): 352—56.

1977 Comini, Alessandra. "For Whom the Bell Tolls; Private versus Universal Grief in the Work of Edvard Munch and Käthe Kollwitz." *Arts* 51 (March 1977): 142.

1978 Feist, P. H. "Die Bedeutung der Arbeiterklasse für den Realismus der Käthe Kollwitz." Reprinted in P. H. Feist. *Künstler, Kunstwerk und Gesellschaft.* Fundus-Bücher, 51—52). Dresden: 1978. Pp. 201—26.

Works: Publications Edited or Authorized by Kollwitz

1913 Kollwitz, Käthe. *Käthe Kollwitz Mappe.* Edited by the Kunstwart. Munich: G.D.W. Callwey, 1913. Issued in portfolio. Revised 1925, 1927, and 1931.

1920 Kollwitz, Käthe. *Handzeichnungen in originalgetreuen Wiedergaben.* Dresden: Emil Richter, 1920. Issued in portfolio containing an original lithograph.
Kollwitz, Käthe. *24 Handzeichnungen in originalgetreuen Wiedergaben.* Preface by W.G. Hartmann. Dresden: Emil Richter, 1920. Issued with an original lithograph.

1922 Kollwitz, Käthe. *Käthe Kollwitz' "Bauernkrieg."* By Theodor Volbehr. Magdeburg: Kaiser-Friedrich-Museum, 1922.

1924 Kollwitz, Käthe. *Abschied und Tod. 8 Zeichnungen von Käthe Kollwitz.* Foreword by Gerhard Hauptmann. Berlin: Propyläen-Verlag, 1924. Limited edition of 300 copies; special edition of 100 copies containing an original lithograph.
Kollwitz, Käthe. *Sieben Holzschnitte zum Krieg.* Dresden: Emil Richter, 1924. 7 original woodcuts issued in portfolio.

1925 Kollwitz, Käthe. *Aus dem Käthe Kollwitz Werk. Mit einem Brief von Käthe Kollwitz an A. Bonus.* Introduction by Hildebrand Gurlitt. Dresden, 1925. Limited edition of 100 copies containing an original signed lithograph.

1927 Kollwitz, Käthe. *Das Käthe Kollwitz Werk.* Introduction by Arthur Bonus. Dresden: Carl Reissner, 1927. Rev. ed., 1930. A limited edition of 100 copies also issued containing an original signed lithograph.
Kollwitz, Käthe. *Ein Weberaufstand. Bauernkrieg. Krieg. Die drei Folgen der Künstlerin.* Edited by Louis Diel. Berlin: Furche-Kunstverlag, 1927.

1932 Kollwitz, Käthe. *Die graphische Kunst von Käthe Kollwitz. 28 Wiedergaben nach Radierungen, Lithographien und Handzeichnungen mit einer biographischen Einleitung nach Angaben der Künstlerin.* Berlin-Charlottenburg: A. von der Becke, c.1932.

1933 Kollwitz, Käthe. *Das neue Kollwitz-Werk.* Dresden: Carl Reissner, 1933.

Works: Other Editions of Kollwitz's Works

Kollwitz, Käthe. *Drawings.* N.p., n.d. 9 plates in portfolio.
Kollwitz, Käthe. *Sei Opere Grafiche dal 1897 al 1909.* Presentazione Antonio Del Guercio. Rome, n.d.

193? Kollwitz, Käthe. *Six Woodcuts.* Newark, N.J: Facsimile Editions, 193?.

1932 Kollwitz, Käthe. *Het werk van Käthe Kollwitz.* Bevattende 61 Reproducties in zwart en wit naar Etsen, Litho's Teekeningen, Houtsneden en Plastieken. Introduction by W. Jos. de Gruyter. The Hague: De Baanbreker/N.V. Servire, 1932.

194? Kollwitz, Käthe. *Kollwitz.* New York: F. Ungar, 194?. 10 plates in portfolio.

1941 Kollwitz, Käthe. *Ten Lithographs.* Introduction by Elizabeth McCausland. Henry C. Keeman, Curt Valentin, 1941.

1947 Kollwitz, Käthe. *10 Radierungen und Lithographien in originalgetreuen Wiedergaben.* Berlin: A. von der Becke, 1947.

1948 Kollwitz, Käthe. *83 Wiedergaben.* Edited with introduction by Fritz Schmalenbach. Bern: Renaissance-Verlag (H. Engeler), 1948.
Kollwitz, Käthe. *Einundzwanzig Zeichnungen der späten Jahre.* Introduction by Carl Georg Heise. Berlin: Gebr. Mann, 1948. Second edition, 1966.
Kollwitz, Käthe. *Ten Reproductions of Lithographs and Woodcuts.* Published with the cooperation of the Tribune Subway Gallery. Touchstone Portfolios: Artists of the People, 4. New York: Touchstone Press, 1948.

1953 Kollwitz, Käthe. *Ein Herz schlägt für die Mütter. 100 Handzeichnungen von Käthe Kollwitz.* Text by Werner Schumann. Hannover: Fackelträger-Verlag, 1953.

1958 Kollwitz, Käthe. *Bauernkrieg.* Introduction by Heinz Mansfield. Dresden: Verlag der Kunst, 1958.

1959 Kollwitz, Käthe. *Drawings.* Edited by Herbert Bittner. New York and London: Thomas Yoseloff, 1959.

196? Kollwitz, Käthe. *Das graphische Werk.* Sammlung Helmut Goedeckemeyer. Braunschweig: Kunstverein Braunschweig, 196?.

1960 Kollwitz, Käthe. *Sechs Lithographien.* Berlin-Halensee: A. von der Becke, 1960.
Kollwitz, Käthe. *Ein Weberaufstand.* Berlin-Halensee: A. von der Becke, 1960.
Kollwitz, Käthe. *Der Weberaufstand.* Introduction by Friedrich Ahlers-Hestermann. Reclams Universal Bibliothek, 9055. Stuttgart: Reclam, 1960.

1967 Kollwitz, Käthe. *The Drawings of Käthe Kollwitz*. Introduction by Stephen Longstreet. Alhambra, Calif.: Border Pub. Co., 1967.
Kollwitz, Käthe. *Das plastische Werk*. Edited by Dr. Hans Kollwitz. Preface by Leopold Reidemeister. Photos by Max Jacoby. Hamburg: Christian Wagner Verlag, 1967.

1969 Kollwitz, Käthe. *Prints and Drawings of Käthe Kollwitz*. Selected with introduction by Carl Zigrosser. New York: Dover Publications, 1969.

1970 Kollwitz, Käthe. *Twenty-one Late Drawings*. Boston: Boston Book & Art, 1970.

Catalogues Raisonnés: Prints

1913 Sievers, Johannes. *Die Radierungen und Steindrücke von Käthe Kollwitz innerhalb der Jahre 1890 bis 1912. Ein beschreibendes Verzeichnis*. Dresden: Hermann Holst (Kunsthandlung Emil Richter), 1913.

1927 Wagner, A. *Die Radierungen, Holzschnitte und Lithographien von Käthe Kollwitz. Eine Zusammenstellung der seit 1912 entstandenen graphischen Arbeiten in chronologischer Folge*. Dresden: Emil Richter, 1927.

1955 Klipstein, August. *Käthe Kollwitz. Verzeichnis des graphischen Werkes für die Jahre 1980–1912 unter Verwendung des 1913 erschienenen Oeuvrekataloges von Johannes Sievers*. Bern: Gutekunst & Klipstein, 1955.
Klipstein, August. *The Graphic Work of Kaethe Kollwitz*. Complete illustrated catalogue, compiled by A. Klipstein. New York: Galerie St. Etienne, 1955

Catalogues Raisonnés: Drawings

1972 Nagel, Otto. *Käthe Kollwitz: die Handzeichnungen*. Edited by Otto Nagel, with the collaboration of Sibylle Schallenberg-Nagel and the advice of Dr. Hans Kollwitz. Scholarly edition by Dr. Werner Timm. Berlin: Henschelverlag Kunst und Gesellschaft, 1972.
Negel, Otto. *The Drawings of Käthe Kollwitz*. With the collaboration of Sibylle Schallenberg-Nagel and Hans Kollwitz. Edited by Werner Timm. New York: Crown Publications, 1972.

Exhibition Catalogues

Buchholz Gallery, Curt Valentin, New York. *Käthe Kollwitz. Drawings, Lithographs, Sculpture*. N.Y., n.d.
College Art Association. *Drawings and Prints by Kaethe Kollwitz from a Private Collection*. Worcester, Massachusetts, n.d. Foreword by Francis Henry Taylor.

1917 Paul Cassirer Galerie, Berlin. *Katalog der Sonderausstellung: Käthe Kollwitz zu ihrem fünfzigsten Geburtstag*. Berlin: Cassirer, 1917. Introduction by Max Deri.

1925 Civic Club, New York City. *Exhibition of Etchings, Woodcuts and Posters by Professor Käthe Kollwitz*, Dec. 20, 1925–Jan. 3, 1926. New York, 1925. Program by Louise Diel.

1938 Kleemann Galleries, New York. *Exhibition. A Choice Collection of Rare Etchings, Woodcuts, Lithographs by Käthe Kollwitz*. New York, 1938.

1946 Augustinermuseum, Freiburg im Breisgau. *Käthe Kollwitz zum Gedächtnis*, December 1946. Baden-Baden: Woldemar Klein, 1946. Introduction by Hanna Kronberger-Frentzen.

Berner Kunstmuseum. *Gedächtnisausstellung Käthe Kollwitz*, May 5–June 30, 1946. Bern, 1946. Text by Fritz Schmalenbach.

1947 The Renaissance Society, University of Chicago. *Prints by Kaethe Kollwitz*, February 4–28, 1947. Chicago, 1947.
Universitätsmuseum, Marburg/Lahn. *Käthe Kollwitz. Gedächtnisausstellung*, July-August 1947. Marburg/Lahn, 1947. Text by Jördis Kollwitz.
Boymans Van Beuningen Museum, Rotterdam. *Herdenkingstentoonstelling, Käthe Kollwitz, 1867–1945*, Aug. 27–Oct. 1, 1947. Rotterdam, 1947.
Zeitlin & Ver Brugge, Los Angeles. *Kaethe Kollwitz Exhibition*, Oct. 29–Nov. 29, 1947. Los Angeles, 1947. Introduction by Jacob Zeitlin.

1948 Kunstmuseum, Winterthur. *Gedächtnis-Ausstellung Käthe Kollwitz 1867–1945*, May 9–June 13, 1948. Winterthur, 1948.
Sonnenhalde Künstlerhaus, Württembergischer Kunstverein, Stuttgart. *Käthe Kollwitz*, September-October 1948. Stuttgart, 1948. Text by E. Petermann.

1950 Gutekunst & Klipstein, Bern. *Käthe Kollwitz. Handzeichnungen. Graphik*. Lagerkatalog 47. Bern, 1950.

1951 Deutsche Akademie der Künste, Berlin. *Käthe Kollwitz. Ausstellung*, March 8–April 29, 1951. Berlin, 1951. Text by Willy Kurth.

1952 Staatliche Graphische Sammlung, München. *Käthe Kollwitz. Zeichnungen und Graphik*, Nov. 19, 1952–Jan. 31, 1953. Munich: Prestel, 1953. Introduction by P. Halm.

1955 Alex Vömel Galerie, Düsseldorf. *Ausstellung Käthe Kollwitz. Das plastiche Werk*, April 22–May 31, 1955. Düsseldorf, 1955.

1956 Fanning, Robert J. *Kaethe Kollwitz*. Karlsruhe: C.F. Müller, 1956. Published in conjunction with Kollwitz exhibition in Amerika Häuser in West Germany.
Galerie St. Etienne, New York. *Kaethe Kollwitz (1867—1945). Drawings and Rare Prints*, April-May 1956. New York, 1956.
Neue Galerie der Stadt Linz/Wolfgang Gurlitt Museum. *Käthe Kollwitz. Das graphische Werk. Druckgraphik. Zeichnungen*, April-May 1956. Linz, 1956. Texts by Walter Kasten and Otto Mauer.

1957 Lange Museum Haus. *Käthe Kollwitz. Gedächtnisausstellung zum 90. Geburtstag, 8.7.1967–22.4.1945*, June-July 1957. Krefeld, 1957.

1958 Municipal Art Galleries, Barnsdall Park, Los Angeles, California. *Kaethe Kollwitz. 25 Masters*, March 4–23, 1958. Los Angeles, 1958.
Smith College Museum of Art, Northampton, Massachusetts. *Kollwitz. Catalogue of the Exhibition and Collection of Thirty-Four Prints and One Drawing*, November 1958. Northampton, 1958. Essay by Leonard Baskin.
Staatliches Museum, Schwerin. *Käthe Kollwitz Ausstellung. Der Schweriner Besitz*, November-December 1958. Schwerin, 1958.

1959 Hans Thoma-Gesellschaft, Spendhaus, Reutlingen. *Käthe Kollwitz*, April 26–May 24, 1959. Reutlingen, 1959. Texts by Hagenlocher and K.A.R.
Galerie St. Etienne, New York. *Kaethe Kollwitz; Drawings, Posters, Rare Prints*, Jan. 12–Feb. 7, 1959. New York, 1959.

1960 Albertinum, Kupferstich-Kabinett, Dresden. *Käthe Kollwitz; Graphik und Zeichnungen aus dem Dresdener Kupferstich-Kabinett*,

May 28–Oct. 23, 1960. Dresden, 1960. Text by Werner Schmidt.

Galerie St. Etienne, New York. *Kaethe Kollwitz; Sculptures, Drawings,* December 1959–January 1960. New York, 1960.

The Montclair Art Museum, Montclair, New Jersey. *Käthe Kollwitz and her Contemporaries. An Exhibition of Prints from the Collection of Samuel and Edith Rosenbaum,* October 2–23, 1960. Montclair, N.J., 1960.

1961 Bernard Hall, James Room, Barnard College, New York. *Loan Exhibition of Etchings. Lithographs and Woodcuts by Kaethe Kollwitz,* Nov. 13–Dec. 4, 1961. New York, 1961. Exhibition from collections of Mr. and Mrs. Abe Lerner and Miss Judith Lerner.

Galerie St. Etienne, New York. *Kaethe Kollwitz (1867–1945); Sketch and Finished Work, Drawings, Rare Prints.* Nov. 11–Dec. 9, 1966. New York, 1961.

1962 Deutsche Akademie der Künste, Berlin. *Käthe Kollwitz; Zeichnungen, Druckgraphik. Ausstellung.* Berlin, 1962. Edited by Helga Weissgärber.

National Gallery of Canada, Ottawa. *Käthe Kollwitz.* Ottawa, 1962. Introduction by Henry Ernest. Exhibit organized and circulated by the National Gallery of Canada.

1963 Duke University, West Alumni Lounge, Durham, North Carolina. *Käthe Kollwitz; Graphic Arts,* March 1–20, 1963. Durham, 1963.

1964 Vancouver Art Gallery. *Käthe Kollwitz.* Vancouver, 1964.

Ernest Raboff Gallery, Los Angeles. *Käthe Kollwitz.* July 20–Aug. 7, 1964. Los Angeles, 1964.

Gesellschaft für Bildende Kunst in Mainz, Haus des Kunstgeschichtlichen Instituts der Johannes Gutenberg-Universität, Mainz. *Käthe Kollwitz. Brot den Armen aller Welt. Radierungen, Lithographien, Zeichnungen und Brozen,* Jan. 14–Feb. 13, 1964. Kleine Schriften der Gesellschaft für Bildende Kunst in Mainz 17. Mainz, 1964. Collection of Helmut Goedeckemeyer.

Jerrold Morris International Gallery Limited, Toronto, Canada. *Käthe Kollwitz. Etchings, Lithographs, Woodcuts, Bronzes,* Oct. 29–Nov. 14, 1964. Toronto, 1964.

1965 Galerie St. Etienne, New York. *Kaethe Kollwitz; Drawings,* May-June 1965. New York, 1965.

Pels-Leusden Galerie, Berlin. *Käthe Kollwitz,* April 25–Aug. 15, 1965. Berlin, 1965.

Staatliches Museum, Berlin. *Käthe Kollwitz.* Berlin, 1965. Text by Werner Timm and Ilse Rauhut.

Main Street Galleries, Chicago. *The Art of Kaethe Kollwitz (1867–1945). 61 Drawings and Signed Prints,* March 8–April 10, 1965. Chicago, 1965.

1967 Akademie der Künste, Berlin. *Käthe Kollwitz, 1867–1945. Eine Ausstellung der Akademie der Künste in Verbindung mit den Staatlichen Museen Preussischer Kulturbesitz Kupferstichkabinett und Nationalgalerie vom Dezember 1967 bis zum 7 Januar 1968.* Berlin, 1967. Edited by Herta Elisabeth Killy, Peter Hahlbrock, and Walter Huder.

Bethnal Green Museum, London. *Käthe Kollwitz. Engravings, Drawings, Sculpture.* London, 1967. Introduction by Kurt Martin. Organized by the German Art Council (Deutscher Kunstrat).

Boymans Van Beuningen Museum, Rotterdam. *Käthe Kollwitz, 1867–1967. Herdenkingstentoonstelling,* Aug. 12–Oct. 8, 1967. Rotterdam, 1967.

Ernst Barlach Haus, Hamburg. *Käthe Kollwitz in ihrer Zeit.* Hamburg, 1967. Catalogue by Isa Lohmann-Siems.

Galerie St. Etienne, New York. *Käthe Kollwitz: In the Cause of Humanity.* New York, 1967.

Goethe-Institut, Paris. *Käthe Kollwitz. Art Graphique, Dessins, Sculptures.* Paris, 1967. Organized by the German Art Council (Deutscher Kunstrat) on the occasion of the artist's centennial. Catalogue by Dr. Ernest Thiele.

Museum Carolino Augusteum, Salzburg. *Zeichnungen und Druckgraphiken, zur Verfügung gestellt von der Deutschen Akademie der Künste zu Berlin.* July-August 1967. Salzburg, 1967. Catalogue by Helga Weissgärber. Edited by Franz Fuhrmann. Introduction by Otto Nagel.

Nationalmuseum, Stockholm. *Käthe Kollwitz. Grafik, Techningar, Skulpturer.* Stockholm, 1967. Organized by the Deutscher Kunstrat.

Overbeck-Gesellschaft, Lübeck. *Käthe Kollwitz. Das graphische Werk. [Sammlung Helmut Goedeckemeyer] Anlässlich des 100. Geburtstages,* June 11–Aug. 6, 1967. Lübeck, 1967. Edited with text by Hans-Friedrich Geist and Friedrich Ahlers-Hestermann. Also shown at Kunstverein Braunschweig, Sept. 3–Oct. 29, 1967.

Städtisches Museum, Bielefeld. *K. Kollwitz, 1967–1945,* July 8–Aug. 6, 1967. Bielefeld, 1967.

Von der Becke, A. *Käthe Kollwitz. Handzeichnungen und graphische Seltenheiten,* July 8–Aug. 5, 1967. Munich, 1967.

Staatsgalerie, Graphische Sammlung, Stuttgart. *Die Zeichnerin Käthe Kollwitz. Ausstellung zum 100. Geburtstag,* October-November 1967. Stuttgart, 1967. Introduction and biography by Gunther Thiem.

Frankfurter Kunstkabinett, Frankfurt am Main. *Käthe Kollwitz,* Nov. 30–Dec. 23, 1967. Frankfurt am Main, 1967.

1968 Boerner, C.G., Antiquariat, Düsseldorf. *Käthe Kollwitz, 1867–1945,* October 1–20, 1968. Düsseldorf, 1968.

Museum of Art, Connecticut University. *Käthe Kollwitz: Prints and Drawings; the Landauer Collection,* Storrs, Conn., 1968. Introduction by Joseph J. Kuntz.

Kunstforening, Bergen. *Käthe Kollwitz, Grafikk, Tegninger, Skulpturer.* Berlin, 1968. Also shown at Stavanger Kunstforening (1968); Tromsø Kunstforening (1968); Trondhjems Kunstforening, Trondheim (1968); Kunstnernes Hus, Oslo (1968).

Marlborough-Gerson Gallery. *Ernst Barlach and Käthe Kollwitz,* September-October 1968. New York, 1968. Text by Alfred Werner.

1969 Galleri 27, Oslo. *Käthe Kollwitz. Grafikk,* Sept. 25–Oct. 19, 1969. Oslo, 1969.

Perocco, Guido. *Mostra di Käthe Kollwitz.* Venice: Sala Napoleonica, 1969.

1970 Peter Deitsch Fine Arts Inc., New York. *Käthe Kollwitz; Rare Prints and Drawings,* February 1970. Stock Catalogue 14; N.S., 2. New York, 1970. Text by Peter H. Deitsch.

1971 Tel Aviv Museum. *Kaethe Kollwitz; Zeichnungen, Radierungen, Lithographien, Holzschnitte, Skulpturen,* Nov. 8–Dec. 11, 1971. Tel Aviv, 1971. Also shown at Israel Museum Dec. 14, 1971–Jan. 21, 1972. Text in Hebrew, English, and German.

1973 Kunstverein, Frankfurt am Main. *Käthe Kollwitz,* June 3–Aug. 12, 1973. Frankfurt, 1973. Also shown at Wurttembergischer Kunstverein, Stuttgart, Sept. 29–Oct. 28, 1973; Neue Gesellschaft für Bildende Kunst, Berlin, Jan. 22–Feb. 28, 1974. Edited by Georg Bussmann.

Wallraf-Richartz-Museum, Cologne. *Käthe Kollwitz; Zeichnungen,*

July 27—Sept. 2, 1973. Cologne, 1973. Catalogue by Hella Robels and Horst Keller.
Minnesota Museum of Art. *Kollwitz; an Exhibition of Graphic Works by Käthe Kollwitz from the Permanent Collection of the Minnesota Museum of Arts,* Sept. 26—Nov. 10, 1973. St. Paul, 1973.

1975   Stanford University Museum of Art. *Käthe Kollwitz: The Graphic Work, a Checklist of the Exhibition.* Nov. 19,1974—Jan. 19, 1975. Palo Alto, Calif., 1975.

1976   Galerie St. Etienne, New York. *Käthe Kollwitz. Exhibition.* December 1—31, 1976, at Kennedy Galleries. New York: Galerie St. Etienne and Kennedy Galleries, 1976.

1977   Museum Villa Stuck, Munich. *Käthe Kollwitz: Zeichnungen, Graphik, Plastik.* May 12—August 7, 1977. Munich, 1977. Catalogue by Amelie Ziersch.

1977—78   Institute for Foreign Cultural Relations, Stuttgart. *Käthe Kollwitz: Engravings, Drawings, Sculpture.* Stuttgart, 1977—78. Text by Uwe M. Schneede.

1978   University Art Galleries, University of California, Riverside. *Käthe Kollwitz, 1867—1945: Prints, Drawings, Sculpture.* April 2—May 5, 1978. Riverside, Calif., 1978. Catalogue by Françoise Forster-Hahn and Kirk deGooyer. Exhibit organized by graduate students in the Department of Art History, University of California, Riverside.

PHOTO CREDITS

It is not the intention of this volume to put any particular interpretation on Käthe Kollwitz's work or to enlist it in support of any particular political position. Humanism is the hallmark of her work, and it was the force that motivated her, with ever increasing intensity as she gained more and more experience of life, to speak out on behalf of the suffering and exploited working people who supplied her with the major motifs of her work.

This book does not lay claim to completeness or profess to make a definitive statement. Its focus is on those themes in Kollwitz's work that are particularly relevant today and offer the contemporary reader ready points of reference in his own experience. Because this volume has been limited to Kollwitz's prints, posters, and the preliminary studies for them, we feel that another volume is in order, one that will include her sculpture and drawings as well as substantial excerpts from the journal she began keeping in 1908.